STALKING NIRVANA

THE NATIVE AMERICAN (RED PATH) ZEN WAY

REV. DUNCAN SINGS-ALONE, SENSEI

Stalking Nirvana
The Native American (Red Path) Zen Way
All Rights Reserved.
Copyright © 2013 Rev. Duncan Sings-Alone, Sensei
v3.0

Cover Illustration by Robin Gulack. © 2013 Two Canoes Press. All rights reserved - used with permission.

ISBN: 978-1-929590-20-9

Library of Congress Control Number: 2013944184

PRINTED IN THE UNITED STATES OF AMERICA

To Roshi Paul Genki Kahn
and Sensei Monika Seiryo Brunner
for their vision of Zen in America.

TABLE OF CONTENTS

"Grandfathers, what do I teach?"

The Grandfathers answered, "Teach people how to live in

harmony with themselves, with each other, and Grandmother Earth.

People are out of balance. Teach them to live in the spirit of

Mitakuye Oyas'in (all my relations), to live in awareness

of our Oneness with all creation. Teach them the true meaning of

Walking in Beauty."

Duncan Sings-Alone

BACKWORD

"Therefore, reverse the intellectual practice of investigating words and chasing after talk; take the backward step of turning the light and shining it back. Of themselves body and mind will drop away, and your original face will appear. If you want such a state, urgently work at zazen." – Dogen Zenji, "Universal Recommendation of Zazen for All (Fukan Zazengi)."

This "Backword" is not merely a wink at Duncan Sings-Alone, one of my Dharma Successors, Founder of Red Path (Native American) Zen, and the author of <u>Sprinting Backwards to God</u>, but a paean to his willingness, after a lifetime of practice and teaching Native American spiritual traditions and Western Psychotherapy, to back up, enter Zen Buddhism and begin from point zero yet again. Perhaps it is no accident that the entrances to the Sweat Lodge (Inipi), to the Zen tea hut, and to the Zen training hall all require bowing down to gain entry. As Dogen Zenji beckoned, Sings-Alone has followed.

This is also an encouragement to you, Reader, to take this backward step yourself. This telling is so deep, you are entering a realm where truth and mythos merge, where lived and dreamed entwine, where incarnation and embodiment are matters of shape-shifting, as a blade of grass manifests the 16-foot golden body of the Buddha, and the 16-foot golden body of the Buddha appears as a mound of Buffalo dung and a constellation of stars. But stand advised, I have witnessed all you will find within these pages, or spent time with those who have. Like "The Heart of the Perfection of Wisdom Sutra," this text "is true, not a lie."

"If you meet a Buddha on the road, kill him!" – Zen Aphorism

Well, that not withstanding, when I meet a Buddha on the road, I invite her or him to walk with me for a bit. And that's how it was when I met Grandfather Duncan Sings-Alone. One wayfarer can recognize another, but don't expect a Buddha to look all Buddha-like. This one's nearly six feet tall and a big guy, handsome, even in his seventies, broad featured and raw-boned, a strong jaw, but gentle in manner, soft and gentle. He's given to jeans, two-tone western shirts and work boots. Most often you can recognize him by a neckerchief he wears as a bandana around his head and his long, silver ponytail. He loves working on the land, and is entirely comfortable with a chainsaw and log-splitter, tractor and hedger.

I don't know how this fellow got through the 10 Bhumis, the stages of a Bodhisattva becoming a Buddha, as delineated in the Flower Garland (Avatamsaka) Sutra, teachings sacred to my spiritual Order. I do know he shows the six signs of a Buddha: moral and ethical Integrity, that respects the intricate diversity and interrelationships of all creation; constant Effort for the wellbeing of all creation; Patience that moves at the organic pace each and everything unfolds; Generosity of spirit, sharing all his resources, knowledge, care, healing arts, property, family and finances; access to the plenitude of Oneness; and Wisdom embodied in breadth of vision and appropriateness of action.

This is a cultured dude, nonetheless. He's well read, holds a PhD in psychology, pioneered in the treatment of what was once called Multiple Personality Disorder. He has a past life as an ordained Christian minister and trained choirmaster. He's a writer and a nationally recognized master storyteller. You'll find him with his novelist wife, Priscilla Cogan, at plays, classical and folk concerts, fingering The Great American Song Book on his piano, or leading a service at his local Unitarian Universalist Center.

Mostly, though, he likes long rambles through woodlands and rocky ranges. Or sitting, legs folded before a blanket and buffalo skull praying with his sacred pipe (Chanupa) and communing with spirits. He has been touched by the Thunder Beings and holds the Vajra thunderbolt; the power one can feel in his ceremonies, his shamanistic channeling of information, his healing work and his presence.

He's a man given to strong spirits, though the vintage is more ancient than most of us can access. He speaks directly with Spirit Guides, and can see them as vividly as you might see me. He has a long relationship with six such Grandfathers, and invokes and praises them in all his work. Take caution, however: Coyote also always accompanies him, and never strays far. Sings-Alone not only gets his sense of humor from that animal, but also has the trickster's skills in teaching. The Lotus Sutra called it "upaya," a mastery of creative approaches to guiding the reluctant and deluded toward awakening, whether they know or not. It is a teaching form present in many traditions, Zen, Tibetan, Sufi, Native American, and has been known as crazy wisdom.

Illuminative and synchronistic events seem to abound when one is with Sings-Alone. Early in our relationship when he had just given me a social pipe with which to practice Chanupa ceremony alone, we took a walk near my home in the High Mountain Preserve that overlooks Franklin Lake, which the Indians had called Crystal Lake. I had walked those woods since childhood, and they gave first name to my spiritual clan, High Mountain Crystal Lake Zen Community. But only walking with Sings-Alone did deer come out to stare at us and the body of a full-grown spotted hawk appear at my feet. Feathers from that hawk now adorn my practice pipe.

" ...when you meet with a man of knowledge, you distinguish what's appropriate to the occasion, you know what's right and what's wrong, and together you witness each other's illumination."

– Yuan Wu, Preface to Case 8, The Blue Cliff Record.

His Spirit Guides cast Sings-Alone out of the Sweat Lodge to warn non-Native peoples that our rape of the Earth and the fabric of its atmosphere were leading to dire consequences, perhaps the extinction of humankind. He was to share that message and teach and lead others back to ways of respect and preservation of the Grandmother. He created a workshop combining the apocalyptic prophesies with Native American teachings on how to relate to Earth and her creatures. I invited him to present his workshop at the Zen institution I was running, and I attended his workshop myself.

He was transmitting a way of oneness that allowed deep communion with nature. I'm talking about teaching urbanites how to really experience a living, sensual kinship with trees, rocks, animals. I recognized this as a mastery of the power of absorption (samadhi), skillfully controlled through awakened mindbody, and directed in a unified field (joriki). This was the province of Zen training, but coming from very different practices and with a total emphasis on our world in form, as well as in spirit.

He told me that he had meditated throughout his life, but only since losing the Sweat Lodge had he begun a more consistent and formal practice of Zen meditation (zazen). His gentle, humble way, vast knowledge and experience, great heart and good humor make him irresistible to folks, and I too fell under his sway. He began practicing Zen with me, attending our retreats and exploring in discussion with me similarities and differences between our paths.

He and his talented wife opened their home to me and began teaching me their Lakota tradition. Priscilla Cogan is a writer, now moving from novels to playwriting. I do want to recommend her trilogy that explores in fiction Native ways and their encounter with modern "civilization": Winona's Web, Compass of the Heart, and Crack at Dusk: Crook of Dawn.

Priscilla is also known by her Lakota name, Buffalo Woman, and is a Water-Pourer empowered to direct Sweat Lodge, and she is experienced in Vision Quests (Hanblecheya). She and Duncan have led and inspired spiritual communities across the United States. They have kept their home and land open to practitioners for decades. For me, their loving, humor-filled relationship is a powerful teaching.

When I met them, they had a Sweat Lodge on their property in Massachusetts. Their daughter, Nancielee Holbrook, called Atsila Gaia, a water-pourer for many years, had agreed to take over leader-ship of Grandfather's Sweat Lodge since the spirits would no longer allow him to sweat. The winter had been rough on the lodge, and Sings-Alone directed us in building a new lodge. He led us in sacred songs and special rituals as we dug a fire pit, gathered 16 saplings, offering tobacco to their stumps, slanted them into the earth, bent and bound them together, and covered it in blankets and a tarp. That structure lasted several years until Super Storm Sandy. This spring we will build another lodge on the property in Massachusetts and one in Airmont, New York, on the grounds of the Zen Garland Sanctuary.

As Sings-alone and I each entered the other's tradition, something new was smelting in the fire and being forged through our efforts. We call this Red Path (Native American) Zen. This is not some integration, a mixing of elements that in truth do not blend. Red Path is founded in both traditions, true to their transmissions and concerns, and is emerging as a New Way on its own terms. This is not a finished or clear course, so we can only invite you to join us on this quest into the unknown. Fall backward into the creative volcano of this very moment. Wrestle with this dragon, soar on the back of an eagle. Take a backward step onto the Red Path and join us in Stalking Nirvana.

Roshi Paul Genki Kahn. Spiritual Director
Zen Garland Order
Airmont, NY

ACKNOWLEDGMENTS

There is no way that I can adequately thank the many people who have taught, guided, and cajoled me on my spiritual journey from which came this book. These are the ones to whom I am most indebted: Rolling Thunder who first called me to the Red Road and George Whitewolf who was my teacher for seven wonderful years. My thanks also to the participants in my various sweatlodge communities. You confirmed my vocation and welcomed my teaching.

My deep appreciation goes to Roshi Paul Genki Kahn, Founder of Zen Garland: A Community and Order for Zen Practice, Education, and Service, who saw value for Zen in the practices of the Red Road. He is an excellent teacher and holds a clear and beautiful vision of Zen in the western world. I am honored that he chose me to be a Dharma Successor. My thanks and admiration to Rev. Monika Seiryo Brunner, Sensei, a fellow Dharma Successor of Roshi Genki, who runs Zen Garland and has assisted me in learning the ways of Zen and its priesthood.

Priscilla Cogan, who is not a Zen Buddhist, nevertheless continues to be a most loving and provocative friend and wife. She refuses to hear my easy explanations or enjoy any of my insurgent pomposity. Priscilla is my constant support, a deeply beloved wife . . . and she laughs at my stories.

Finally, my deep gratitude to my constant Spirit guide and teacher, Grandfather Ishnala Mani. He seems to be as comfortable working with a Zen priest and Sensei as he was in working with a medicine teacher. He brings equal parts laughter and gravity.

Duncan Sings-Alone

PREFACE*

Every end always signals a beginning.

Today, wrapped in a towel, eagle wing in hand, I called the Grandfather Spirits for a sweatlodge, inipi, ceremony. A cool, winter breeze carried the call of my eagle bone whistle to the sky. Smoke from the sacred fire flavored the air. My heart surged in eager antici-pation. Crouching, I entered the Lodge and crawled around the stone pit to my seat by the door. Longman, Gentle Spirit, and Priscilla fol-lowed. For now, this is the way I prefer to pray, surrounded by a small group of loved ones.

The lodge exuded the familiar musty smell of blankets long ex-posed to the elements. Settling down, cross-legged before the pit, I arranged my rattles, antlers, sage, sweet grass, and cedar. Overhead, hung my Stoneman and tobacco ties. The eagle wing lay at my side.

"Inyan!" I called for the red hot stones. One by one the Grandfather stones were brought by pitchfork and placed into the pit by our feet. Finally, the door keeper passed a bucket of water into the Lodge and sealed the flap. Home again, in the womb of Grandmother Earth, the deep blackness of the Lodge formed a secure mantel around our shoulders. We sat quietly observing the stones, listening to them, waiting for a sign. Our knees and toes burned from the intense heat.

Ready at last, I sang my Spirit-Calling Song, and began to pour the water which burst into steam, licking our flesh in stinging delight. "Oh Grandfather above. My Grandfathers in all the Directions. Sky

Beings. Grandmother Earth. This is your Grandson, Sings-Alone." The prayers began as they had hundreds of times before in the familiar sweatlodge litany. Peace flooded our hearts as we released the poisons and pettiness perverting our spirits.

Outside the inipi's shelter, a new world was being born, a New Age of incredible spiritual chaos and hope. The Indian world continued to be ripped by fierce quarrels over who is a real Indian, and who has a right to ceremony in traditional ways. Labor pains are seldom pleasant. Having followed the Spirits' directives to the best of my abilities, I yearned for quietness, for centering, and for healing a tired soul. It was, and still is, my time to sink into obscurity for a while.

But Coyote curls beside me resting for the next adventure. He is still watching, one eye open!

* The last paragraphs of *Sprinting Backwards to God*
December 1994 - Sings-Alone's place, Mechanicsville, Maryland
Duncan Sings-Alone

PART ONE

FROM THE RED ROAD
TO RED PATH ZEN

CHAPTER **1**

HOW IT ALL BEGAN

Before encountering Red Path Zen, let's look at the previous thousand miles. It began at White Wolf's Paradise, the home of my teacher.

Once you turned off the road onto George Whitewolf's driveway, you braced yourself for a bumpy, chaotic drive. The holes were big enough to swallow a horse. If you slid too far to the right, you would be mired in an overgrown field so you hugged the left side, praying that your tires wouldn't get buried in mud. At the end of the driveway, cars were parked in haphazard fashion.

Whitewolf's house was long past needing paint. The skeleton of a new addition had been nailed onto the old home. The house was worn, ragged, warm, and comfortable.

Making your way up to the house was an added challenge as you balanced on boards laid precariously over mud holes. Climbing the stone and concrete steps, you proceeded carefully over the porch, wary of missing boards. Finally you stepped through the open door into the space that served as both living room, work room, dining room and kitchen.

There was time before each sweatlodge (inipi) ceremony to visit, drink wokalapi (coffee), and get some teachings from Whitewolf. After a while, everyone headed to the sweatlodge area to split wood and set the fire. It would take two or three hours, again time to visit, smoke our social pipes and make tobacco ties (little pinches of tobacco in tiny red pouches strung on crochet string). These would be hung over our heads during the sweatlodge as offerings to the Spirits. They would carry our prayers and be burned in the following sweatlodge so that all the inipi ceremonies were tied together.

The sweatlodge ceremony takes a couple of hours. Afterwards, the participants, all smelly, dirty and stringy-haired, retire to the house for the post-sweat feast. The room buzzes with conversation and comradery while food is served, and people eat wherever they can find a seat.

Every Thursday and Saturday for seven years, this was my world. I had poured the water for many sweatlodge ceremonies, participated in many more, sometimes six in a single week. Whitewolf put me on the hill four times. During my four-day, four-night vision quest, the Spirits began to work directly with me. It was no surprise that soon after this hamblecheya, Whitewolf announced I would be leaving his community to go build a community of my own. He finally felt either safe enough to turn me loose or glad for the excuse to send me on.

During my hanblecheya the lightning chose me to walk the medicine road. I have thunder medicine meaning that I am a bit Heyoka, the clown, making jokes often during very serious times. At Christmas, Whitewolf would do an inipi ceremony for Christians praying that they would take Jesus more seriously, so that they might behave more honorably toward Indians. At that time I was lead singer in the community. Whitewolf called on me to sing an opening chant in the inipi ceremony. I began with "O Little Town Of Bethlehem" in a pseudo-Indian style. He yelled, "Shut up, Duncan. Spirits going to kill you." But he was chuckling at the same time. I kept his community laughing with my off-beat humor.

Out of a mixture of habit and affection, I continued to show up at Whitewolf's "Paradise" every week, and he continued to announce that I was leaving to form my own community. When he finally gifted me a hand-carved war club made with symbols of both our Medicines, I knew it was time for me to let go and move on.

That night as Priscilla (Buffalo Woman) and I left Whitewolf's Paradise, the last embers of the sweatlodge fire had faded away to wisps of smoke. The dampness and humidity of the sweatlodge still filled the air. It was all so familiar. We could already feel the sadness of leaving our spiritual "home" while we were excited by what was coming next on our spiritual journey.

We knew exactly where to build the inipi, which eventually grew to two inipis, one for men and one for women. We had scouted the territory and were set on the location.

We were living in an Amish community .The Amish folk were used to being watched as objects of curiosity, but now the roles were reversed. As we prepared the sweatlodge fire, the Amish buggies would come clopping down the road, slow down; black bonnets appearing around the buggy walls as the people wondered about these strange new Indians living among them.

Very quickly Buffalo Woman and I built our first inipi (sweatlodge). By chance, a Southern Maryland journalist heard about our plans and wrote a local interest story. A young Potowatomi read it and became the first person to join our lodge. He was followed by a succession of Cherokee, Iroquois, Apache, Anglos, and the journalist. That was twenty-five years ago. A succession of sojourners on the red road, water pourers for the sweatlodge, pipe carriers, vision questers have come from our subsequent lodges.

Nearly all my students have longed to belong to a sacred community, to engage more intensely in prayer, to open more completely to the Sacred, and to feel a connection to Wakan Tanka (Great Mystery).

I have also seen this desire intensify, stoked by the fires of New Age religion. My own spirituality deepened with time and prayer. Grandfather Ishnala Mani and my other Spirit Teachers have been patient with me as I have struggled to learn. They have guided my journey, sometimes with a heavy hand.

CHAPTER 2

STORYTELLING

During those early years with Whitewolf, I discovered my love for storytelling. All Indian tribes cherish and pass on their collections of tales which teach their values and cultural traditions. I loved learning and telling the truth in these myths and legends.

Native people did not have written languages. The Cherokees were the first tribe to have one. Interestingly, it was created by the Cherokee, Sequoia, in 1811. He invented a syllabary, not an alphabet, but with his creation, a Cherokee could learn to read his own language in a week's time. Very soon the Cherokees had a national newspaper, The Phoenix, published in parallel columns, Cherokee and English. Later, in the 1800's, missionaries tried to capture the languages of other tribes using the English alphabet. Their efforts often were a hit or miss job, leaving the tribes with inferior translations and no common spelling to this day. Most typically, the written languages are English translations. But these difficulties did not prevent the tribes from preserving their precious oral traditions complete with legends and tales. And so it was that I became a storyteller, for oral stories are much more entertaining, immediate, and memorable than written ones and irreplaceable for passing on the culture.

Even our funniest stories for very young children are important for teaching our values and culture. My father, a Christian minister, was a storyteller, and I have inherited that same talent. Local schools, museums, and adult groups scheduled me regularly

So it was that one morning I found myself in front of a group of first graders sitting on the classroom floor at my feet, wide-eyed, engrossed by the big Indian. I had run through my rabbit and coyote tales, showed some of my artifacts, and now asked if there were questions. A hand shot up in the air. A little girl asked, "Why do you wear all those ribbons?"

She was referring to my ribbon shirt which is "dress up" wear for our people. The shirt features stitched , ribbons hanging in all the rainbow colors. I answered, "We wear these ribbon shirts because we love colors."

"Well," she replied, "*Real* people love colors too." She proceeded to point out all her red, yellow, and green-clad classmates. To these children Indians seemed on the same level as an Easter Bunny, Snow White or Aladdin.

Telling traditional stories to non-native children may not seem like spiritual teaching, but it is very important to help children understand that Indians have always existed and are still here. It was hard for them to make the connection between me and the copper-skinned, black-braided Indians of Hollywood. In the beginning I would wear buckskins for storytelling, but later in my work I stopped wearing the buckskins and dressed "western." Otherwise, I could not get the children beyond thinking of Indians as bygone relics.

Even when I stopped wearing buckskins, I would take Priscilla's and my wedding clothes with me so the children could admire the fully beaded, elk skin outfits. They loved the soft feel of the tanned hides.

If you read my first book, *Sprinting Backwards to God,* you will remember that Whitewolf did not approve my marrying a white woman. He said, "You have to marry back into the people. You are bleached enough already." But he came to love Priscilla, and when it was time for us to marry, he performed the wedding. He was also an artisan in making buckskin clothing. This was the way he supported his family. He agreed to make our wedding clothes.

On our wedding morning as we left the house to walk down to the sweatlodge area, he stepped back, looking at Priscilla and admired his handiwork. He opined, "Now you look like a proper Lakota woman!"

She replied, "I love Duncan and I love this way to pray. But you have to know that I am a proud, Irish-American woman, and under this elk skin I am wearing kelly green underwear.

To which he replied in Lakota, "Wasichu win witko (Crazy White woman.)"

When I would be telling in a school, I would always remind the children to be proud of their heritage. I would then ask them if they could keep a secret. They always assured me they could. I would further caution them that this was a really big secret and if they told, I could get in trouble. By now, they were about to die with eagerness. "Yes. Yes." They could keep my secret.

Then, I would tell them about Priscilla and her green underwear. That was just about the most wonderful secret they had ever heard.

A week or so later, I would typically get a manila folder in the mail containing a bunch of thank you notes, decorated with stick figure drawings depicting a woman in a dress with green underpants.

One afternoon I stopped by a convenience store for coffee. A woman sidled up to me and asked, "Are you that Indian storyteller?" I said that I was. She grinned and said, "I know your secret." Her first grader couldn't wait to get home and spill the beans.

I also love the way children speak the truth as they see it. Oyo Traditions was an African American folk festival in a local college near Baltimore. They wanted an Indian storyteller for the upcoming festival. I was honored to be asked.

On the designated evening, I arrived at the festival auditorium. There had been a series of dancers and speakers honoring the cultural traditions from Africa and the Bahamas. To my amazement, I had a dressing room. Storytellers don't get dressing rooms. Of course, I had to share it with a group of ten year old inner-city boys who were being dressed for their performance of Ghanian dances. Their fathers were carefully wrapping them in their orange and brown regalia. They would follow after me on stage.

One chunky lad watched me with jaundiced eye as I stood by the door waiting for my stage call. Finally he said, "Just who are you?"

I answered that I was the Indian storyteller who would be on stage just before him.

He said, "I don't know who you is, but you ain't no Indian."

His father tried to hush him, embarrassed. I was thoroughly tickled. I knew that in five minutes I would be on stage in front of a thousand Festival goers and they would be thinking, "I don't know who he is, but he ain't no Indian." In their defense I must confess that I am a mixed blood. My father was mostly Scott with a little Cherokee. Mother was mostly Cherokee. She had beautiful dark skin and blue black hair. In appearance, I inherited mostly the Scottish genes.

Children tell it like they see it. God love them.

I was telling stories in a small rural school. Most of the kids lived on farms and they knew all the animals, both domestic and wild. I was well into my Cherokee story of how Rabbit lost his tail and was waxing eloquent about how long and lovely Rabbit's tail had originally been, and how proud Rabbit was of his appendage, when I was distracted by a little boy in the front row. He was hissing quietly to get my attention. When I looked at him, he brought his thumb and pointer finger together and whispered loudly, "Little tail. Little tail." He didn't want the big Indian storyteller to get it wrong.

On another occasion in the late 1980's, dressed all in buckskins and feathers, I was driving south to Leonardtown, Maryland, the county seat, to tell stories for their elementary school classes. It was a divided highway. Up ahead I noticed that a sheriff's car had stopped beside the road. As I drew closer, I saw that the deputy was pointing his handgun at something laying just off the road. An old gentleman was standing beside him.

Slowing down, I saw that a deer laying there that had apparently been hit by a car, and the deputy was preparing to "put it out of its misery."

Making a quick U turn, I pulled up behind the squad car where the two men remained standing, looking at the fallen deer. I switched off the motor, opened my door, grabbed some tobacco, and began to walk toward the officer. You can imagine his double take when he saw an Indian in full buckskin regalia approaching him in a deliberate fashion. As I walked past him toward the deer, I said, "Relax. It's going to be okay."

Kneeling down by the deer whose eyes were beginning to cloud over in death, I gently placed a pinch of tobacco by its nose. This was a gift of respect to a life that had been snuffed way before its time. The officer watched me, slack-jawed, as I nodded and headed back to my car. I wonder how he explained that to his shift supervisor.

Proceeding on to the school, I pulled into the parking lot and began to gather the Native artifacts that I brought to show the children. Inside the school office there was a commotion of which I was blissfully unaware. The PTA president had stormed into the office, ordering them to call the sheriff immediately. "There is an Indian in the parking lot!"

The resource teacher and principal tried to reassure her that it was Dr. Duncan who had come to tell stories to the children.

"I don't care what you call him, there is an Indian in the parking lot. Get the Sheriff."

It was two weeks later before the resource teacher dared tell me about the panic I had caused. The old anti-Indian bigotry and fear still lurks in the hearts of some people.

Years before, Whitewolf had given me a Lakota love flute. It is a regular wooden Indian flute with a mallard duck's head carved on the open end. I love to tell the children about the flute. When a young man falls in love, he takes a love flute and tries to compose a love song in his heart. It will be his very own song and he must learn to play it perfectly.

When he is satisfied with his song, he slips near the girl's tipi. It should be a beautiful, clear night with stars twinkling overhead. He will begin to play his very own love song. If he does it well, if he truly captures the love in his heart and expresses it through the flute, the young woman lying inside the tipi will listen attentively.

As the lovely sound infiltrates her tipi, her heart begins to flutter. Before long she will slide out from under the tipi and join her boyfriend. Very soon, he will face her father asking how many horses are needed for the daughter's hand in marriage. If all goes well, they marry, and there will be a new family in the village.

All this time, I am holding the flute in front of the class. Invariably, some youngster will ask me to play it. I always demur, saying, "I don't dare. If I play the flute, I can't tell what effect it will have on your teacher. It might cause her to do something real embarrassing like come over here and snuggle up to me."

Of course, the kids start yelling, "Do it. Do it."

I keep saying "no." But finally I give in with the stipulation that they keep their eyes on the teacher to make sure that she doesn't do anything to embarrass either of us.

I begin to play.

If the teacher is an old-fashioned "school marm," she will stand firm, arms folded, maintaining her dignity and authority come hell or high water. But if it is a younger, less rigid teacher, she might begin to slide ever so slowly down the wall toward me. The children then howl with laughter. I bet they never forget the story of the Indian love flute.

Once I was telling this story to children in a special school for the hearing impaired. A sign language translator worked with me. After I finished all the stories and was preparing to leave, two little ten-year-old girls came up to me very shyly and began a conversation with the translator.

The translator said, "They want you to know that when you played the flute, their hearts fluttered too."

For people without a written tradition, story was the way of transmitting history, sacred teaching, and everything important about the culture. Storytelling continued to be a basic teaching tool I used with both children and adults even as I moved into the Zen Buddhist world. Of course, there I found that story was essential even though they had a written tradition stretching back 2000 years. Many of the Zen teaching stories took the form of koans with the appearance of riddles that could not be answered logically. "What is the sound of one hand clapping?" "What was your original face before your parent were born?" "Does a dog have a Buddha nature?" These are well known first koans for which intellectual discussion cannot provide an answer. They actually come from the biographies of great Zen masters, their conversations with their students.

CHAPTER **3**

THE MASSACHUSETTS SWEATLODGE

After twenty years in Maryland as psychologists, storytellers, and spiritual teachers, retiring was an easy decision. Priscilla enjoyed early success as a novelist, and wanted to spend full-time writing. Her early "Winona trilogy," which compared the healing traditions and cultural ideas of Native Americana with western Psychology, had won an early following. In addition, having spent 30 years as psychologists in both agency and private practice, we were both ready to do something else. Our sweatlodge community in Southern Maryland had spawned two other inpi communities in the area, so the teaching would continue without our being there.

Moving to Massachusetts was an easy decision. Priscilla had been born in Belmont, a town just outside Boston. She still had childhood friends in the area, and since she was 12 years younger than me, it was highly likely that I would die before her. I wanted to leave her with a support group.

Our first task was to find a house that would be open and large enough to accommodate meetings and feasts for a small sweatlodge community. We would also need a minimum of five acres, private space, in which to build a sweatlodge. In the interest of efficiency,

Priscilla developed a detailed checklist of all that we needed and sent it to Realtors west and northwest of Boston.

After showing us several unacceptable properties, a young realtor said there was one final house that might work for us. Driving down a secluded country lane, she paused at the head of a driveway. It was such a long driveway that we could tell little about the house. From our vantage point, it certainly was a strange looking place with apparently flat roofs but a very high peak over the garage which we discovered held solar-thermal hot water panels.

Once inside, we were delighted with the openness of the house. Its large living room/dining room/kitchen area was perfect for ceremonial meals. The house had been designed by an architect working with the owner, a physics professor, who had wanted the most "green" house that could be designed by 1970's standards for maximum active and passive solar heat, and maximum summer coolness. We wanted this house.

"One other thing," I said. "What size property is this? We will need at least five acres."

The agent answered, "It has thirteen acres."

The house had just come on the market. We made an offer immediately which was accepted the next day. Our Massachusetts home was secured.

Once having settled in, our next task was to build the inipi. Although we had thirteen acres, most of it was wet lands and not suitable for a sweatlodge. We walked and walked over the property through swamp and small sink holes. There were places that would have been very private, but the ground was too uneven and mushy. Finally, we decided upon a spot near the house at the edge of one of our creeks. It was not perfect, but it would do.

Construction of the lodge was our next step. We cut sixteen saplings of just the right height and diameter. Each time a sapling was taken, a pinch of tobacco was left as an offering of respect to the young tree. We had removed it from life in the most respectful way possible and would use it for a sacred purpose. A few smaller saplings were chosen to form the ribs of the lodge. With just the two of us, it was difficult to bend and tie the saplings into the appropriate shape. When finished, the lodge looked something like an igloo, the appropriate shape.

After the lodge was made, we had to prepare an altar for the buffalo skull to hold the sacred pipes (chanupa wakan). Next we cut and installed colored ribbons into the lodge to honor the powers of the sacred directions. We had already collected thirty blankets to cover the lodge, so it was ready to use.

We had no community. We had no contacts with people who might want to sweat. We were depending on the Spirits to guide a potential community to us. If we built the lodge we trusted they would come, and that is exactly what happened

Somehow during the move and lodge building, I managed to pull my back. Someone recommended a chiropractor in a neighboring community. As he adjusted my back, I told him what we were planning. He was immediately interested and asked if he could come. He also mentioned that a colleague, another chiropractor who had Native American blood, would probably be interested. At that point, we were open to anyone who might join us, so I invited both him and his colleague. The sweatlodge community began to take shape.

Within a month, our community was thriving. Occasionally someone would attend only one sweat and realize it was not for them. Others came just a few times, but a core community developed that would remain together through the following years. It had been my goal to have a much smaller community in Massachusetts and to train a few folk who would become pipe carriers and water pourers, able to take my place when I was unavailable.

Over the ensuing years, there were three who were called by the Spirits to become spiritual leaders: Atsila Gaia, Sky Dreamer, and Spirit Singer. I honor them.

CHAPTER 4

NANCIELEE - ATSILA GAIA

The first was Nancielee, the colleague of the chiropractor who treated my back. He had asked to bring her because he knew she was interested in Indian "things" and was of Indian descent.

She came to one of our first inipi ceremonies in the summer of 1997, and really never left. Not wanting to be a passive participant, she looked for ways to help and was eager to accept responsibility.

A sweatlodge community is work-intensive. Wood must be cut, split, and stacked. Stones had to be gathered, and on ceremonial days, there was the fire to be set and maintained. The fires and the stones have to be handled in specific ways. There is a traditional and sacred way to do these things that must be learned. Nancielee was all eyes.

My first teacher, Rolling Thunder, used to say "White people are kind of retarded. You can tell because they only learn by pestering you with questions. If they would keep their eyes open, mouths shut, and watch what is happening, they would learn everything they needed to know." This is usually, but not always, true. Nancielee is Lakota Indian. She paid attention but she also asked a lot of questions.

When this energetic young woman demonstrated her commitment to work, we were delighted. Before long she was learning to be the fire-keeper for ceremonies. It was her job to prayerfully select the right stones, lay the firewood in a special, sacred way, then build and maintain the fire. The Spirits named her Atsila Gaia, Fire Woman.

She was learning by watching. That sometimes resulted in hilarious mistakes.

My staff, crowned by deer antlers, stood to the left of the altar. After making my tobacco ties, I would hang them on the right side of the antlers. Priscilla would put hers on the left. Atsila Gaia was watching, paying attention, and she carefully hung her ties next to Priscilla's. For us, the staff represents my person as both ceremonial and spiritual leader. Only Priscilla has the right to hang her tobacco ties next to mine. This recognizes the physical and spiritual intimacy of our relationship. I had to laugh and tease Atsila Gaia, informing her that she and I didn't have that kind of intimate relationship. She grabbed her ties and put them with the rest of the prayer ties on the buffalo horns. Red with embarrassment, she never made that mistake again.

Several months after being with us, we discovered that she was embroiled in a destructive marriage. She needed a safe place to work through all the issues facing her, so we invited her to come live with us. While with us, she sued for divorce and began a new life. She resided with us for about three years.

She was learning to watch everything, to look for signs, and to respect all the birds and animals that lived around us. There were deer, coyote, many kinds of birds, fisher cats, raccoons, opossums, and snakes.

One afternoon she was in her bedroom working at the computer. I have an artificial crow that looks like the real thing. Slipping out of the house, crouching low, I positioned the crow on a stick outside her window. The next time she looked up, she saw a crow staring intently at her.

Wide-eyed, Atsila Gaia ran into my office, breathlessly telling me about the crow that was watching her. I warned her to be very respectful of the crow, that he was probably bringing her an important message, so she should pay special attention. She slipped back into her bedroom and, sure enough, the crow was still there. She offered tobacco toward him and was being as respectful as possible.

When her back was turned, I moved the crow to another window. Startled, she came running again to say that the crow was now at a different window, just staring. No matter how hard she tried to listen, she couldn't hear the crow say anything.

Finally, having pity, I had her step out of the house and peer around the corner to get a better view. At that point she realized there was something strange about the crow. I had to confess that coyote had been messing with her head. She was beginning to learn the price for living close to someone with coyote spirit.

Coyote is big in the Indian world. Various tribes had their own Trickster spirits. Among the Cherokee it was Rabbit. The Lakota spoke of the spider, Iktomi. Northwest tribes had the Raven. Coyote, though, has become the common trickster archetype throughout the Indian world.

Coyote exists to complete the creative process of the universe. He is often foolish, doing dumb things, but is a very powerful teacher. His lessons can be painful and often humiliating. For instance when President Clinton looked into the camera and proclaimed, "I never had sex with that woman," Indians saw old Coyote with his arm around Clinton's shoulder, saying "Welcome, bro." As someone with a strong coyote spirit, I often find myself teaching in the same vein. Fortunately, Atsila Gaia was able to deal with my teasing, and learned the things necessary to function in this world.

Over the years, she has deepened her practice of Native American spirituality. She developed into a sacred pipe carrier and sweatlodge leader. Atsila Gaia also became a deeply loved member of our personal family. Ultimately, the three of us performed the Hunka ceremony in which Priscilla and I adopted her as our daughter and she adopted us as parents. It was a natural progression.

More than anything she wanted to live close to the Creator and to be a servant of the people. Her desire to be a servant and teacher led her to give up her chiropractic practice and become a corps commander in the Massachusetts Maritime Academy. Her corps of young college students preparing for careers in the Navy and the Merchant Marine became her children into whom she poured the morals and values of the Native American world.

In June 2009, the Mass Maritime Academy sent her to South Dakota for a leadership development program. At one point the venue changed from Rapid City to Spearfish. A friend who had lived on the Pine Ridge Lakota reservation offered to drive Atsila Gaia's rental car for her because she knew the roads. As they journeyed toward Spearfish there was a stalled car on the other side of the road.

Her friend stopped to inquire whether the driver of the disabled car needed help. A pickup truck with a mother driving her teenage son to a ball game was barreling down the road and never saw their car sitting dead ahead. There was no evidence that brakes on the pickup were ever applied. The 65 mph collision smashed the trunk of Atsila Gaia's car into the front seat. Atsila Gaia and her friend were terribly injured. Their survival was a miracle in itself. Atsila Gaia suffered moderate to severe traumatic brain injury which will affect her as long as she lives. Priscilla immediately flew to South Dakota to be with her until she was strong enough to bring her home and begin her rehabilitation.

At that time we were spending the summer in Priscilla's ancestral home in Michigan. The family had bought the land in the late 1800's, and the house was built in 1926. It is a beautiful, old home surrounded by fifty acres of deep northern woods and perched on a bluff 250 ft above Lake Michigan. There is a half mile long driveway connecting the house with the main road.

By the time Priscilla could bring Atsila to Michigan and begin rehabilitation, she was able to walk unsteadily with a walker. The first morning home, Priscilla fastened a wide canvass belt around Atsila's waist, replaced the walker with two walking sticks, and announced they would begin walking to the road and back every day.

Atsila looked at Priscilla like Priscilla had lost her mind. But they started down the drive, Priscilla holding onto the canvas belt and initiated a morning ritual that lasted the rest of the summer. Before long, the belt was discarded and Atsila Gaia was on her own.

The Spirits told Atsila Gaia that the accident would be the transforming experience of her life. While she lost some of her cognitive sharpness, she became more assertive, less inhibited, and more sure of her ability to serve the spiritual needs of the community. At the time of this writing, she has inherited my Sweatlodge community and is becoming a powerful teacher and leader.

When informed that I had written about her, she replied, "Well, make sure you put in there how hot a babe I am; how hot I was when I began sweating, and am even a hotter woman after the accident. Did I mention to say how hot and humble I am?" Coyote has also been stalking her.

CHAPTER 5

MATT - SKY DREAMER

Fall in New England is spectacular. Our new home nestled into a small forest of hardwoods that were rapidly shedding leaves of amazing colors. Sitting in my office in that Fall of 1998, I was pondering the wonder of it all while dreading hours of lawn raking, when the telephone yanked me back into reality. The co-owner of the local New Age book store was calling.

"Sings-Alone, I have a woman here whose child has been sick from age three until now. He is fourteen. Children's Hospital has not been able to diagnose his illness. Not knowing what else to do, she called a psychic in New Mexico who told her to find a Native American medicine man. She is asking me if I know of anyone. I told her that I would call you and see if you were interested in seeing him."

Native people are uncomfortable with the term "medicine man." That is not part of our cultural language and implies a kind of magician or conjurer. Unfortunately, over time we have been stuck with the title but feel a bit awkward using it. French traders who saw our healers as similar to their doctors coined the term. It is true that I am a healer and ceremonialist. I think of myself as a medicine teacher and healer. The idea that this woman was so determined to find help for her son that she would contact a psychic all the way across the country intrigued me. I agreed to see her son the next day.

The following morning, the doorbell rang. I opened it to find a young mother with her fourteen-year-old son in tow. He could best be described as a frail, longhaired, wannabe hippy. He was bent forward in an unnatural concaved posture, unable to stand up straight. As a small child, his body had been bent backwards in a convex manner. I had never seen this problem before.

Matt was cooperative and interested as I prepared the room for a healing ceremony. The Spirits generally guide me during a healing. For this first time, I put him on a massage table. From this elevated position, I could better read his aura and do a straight "hands on" healing. I felt a good connection with him. He experienced the ceremony as very powerful. Afterwards, I invited him to the next sweatlodge ceremony where we could continue his healing in an even more intense way. He was eager to come.

The following Saturday, Matt arrived early, raring to get started. I think he was wearing the same clothes he wore two days earlier. His bare feet were shod in a worn pair of Birkenstock Sandals. He looked totally incongruous in the sweatlodge group where everyone was dressed for fall in blue jeans, long sleeved shirts, and outdoor shoes. But Matt seemed to feel right at home. He immediately expressed an interest in learning everything.

Incidentally, the healing ceremonies worked. Over time he was able to walk upright. He found a place among his peers and developed some deep friendships. Although he could stand straighter, his spine remained problematic. Ultimately, he was diagnosed with Ankylosing Spondylitis, a condition that was making his spine slowly fuse and lose its flexibility. This was accompanied by constant discomfort and, at times, real pain.

After that first sweatlodge, Matt became one of the most steady members of the community. His mind was a sponge for knowledge. Sweatlodges were painful for him, but he was determined to learn everything about the inipi and the sacred pipe.

School was a different story. Only mildly interested in school, he put his heart in the sacred pipe, sweatlodge and everything Indian, as his one ambition was to become a spiritual person.

Matt's second great love was to party. The great storyteller, Ed Stivender, told a story about Pilgrims and Indians. He said that when a Pilgrim approached the pearly gates, St Peter would inquire, "Did you have a good time on earth?"

The Pilgrim would always say, "No, I was very serious. I obeyed all the laws and spiritual precepts and avoided any manner of sin."

St Peter would respond, "Tsk, Tsk. You will have to go to a special reformation room and listen to the retelling of your life a thousand times."

When an Indian showed up at the pearly gates, St. Peter would ask, "Did you have good time."

The Indian would say "Yes, I had a great time. I had fun. I partied when I could and I partied when I couldn't."

St Peter would smile, "Good job . . . Go directly into heaven."

Irish Matt was a perfect Indian. As soon as his back straightened, he began to make friends in his own age group, a wonderful group of kids, 1960's vintage flower children. Unfortunately, Matt also began to experiment with drugs.

Years later I was told by one of his friends, that Matt was always the leader of his group of friends. Sometimes they would party and stay high for four or five days. Matt would always be the one to say, "This is enough. It's time to clean up."

There are strict rules around our ceremonies. You cannot participate in a sweatlodge if you have imbibed any alcohol or used a recreational drug that day. Not once did Matt show up for sweatlodge after drinking or being stoned. Several of our people despaired of Matt ever getting it together. They assumed that he would waste his life drugging, drinking, and coming to sweatlodge every Saturday to clean up. I believed that Matt had wonderful potential and that given an opportunity, he would straighten out his life.

In time, Matt learned to prepare the sweatlodge fire. He would linger over every stone until he knew that it was the right one for that ceremony. He loved to select big stones so that the sweat would be very hot. Everyone else might be burning up, but Matt would be ecstatic. It was never too hot inside the lodge or too cold outside for him. He would be there, even in the snow, wearing his Birkenstock sandals, his ragged jeans, and tie-dyed T shirt.

He loved to do tie-dyes. It was his personal artistic expression. During the post- sweat feast, we would all tease him. With his long brown hair and scraggly beard, he looked just like a tie-dyed clad Jesus down from the cross.

Matt regularly met with me to talk about his plans and concerns. He shared with me his love interests and his frustration with his progress in life. Matt's dream remained to become a healer, and he wanted to "get there" as quickly as possible.

I kept suggesting to him that he might consider community college because even a wicasa wakan (holy man) needed to have some education in the modern world. He grudgingly enrolled in Framingham State University while wondering how he could help his fellow students. Somewhere along the line, Matt gave up drugs. I am sure he smoked marijuana from time to time, but he got rid of the heavier stuff.

One spring was particularly awful for Matt. His mother was dying of a brain cancer, and Matt spent every available moment with her. He was desperate to help her and scoured the Internet for every possible remedy. As summer drew near, Matt asked the Spirits during a sweatlodge ceremony if he could do a one day/night vision quest. He wanted to spend that time praying for his mother.

In our tradition, someone who had grown enough to become a sacred pipe carrier could go on the hill. In our language, this means vision quest. The first time would be for a day and night. Most vision questers only do the one day/one nighter. Some might choose to do a second vision quest for two days and two nights. Very few might choose three days and nights. The only ones attempting the four day four night vision quest were those preparing to walk the medicine road. During the vision quest, men wore only a beach towel around their waist. Women would wear a simple cotton dress. During the time on the hill, there would be no food, water or human contact. It was a time to be alone with the Spirits.

During the first trip to the hill, one hopes to find his/her spiritual name and the identity of his/her plant or animal helpers. This happens fairly often, but it is not guaranteed.

Matt hoped this would be the first of many such ceremonies. We all held our breaths, hoping that Kurt Cobain would not show up as his Spirit Teacher! We didn't know what to expect.

I always camp out at the bottom of vision quest hill, to be there if needed. I do not approach the quester unless the Spirits tell me to take him/her down. The community and I sing sacred songs a couple times during the night. Although not seen, we are heard. Should the quester come down early, he or she is to stop at my tent waking me up so we can immediately put him or her in the sweatlodge, build up the fire, heat stones and do the closing ceremony in which the Spirits interpret the experiences remembered by the vision quester.

The community followed Matt up to the vision quest altar, gave him a hug and departed. Later that night, I crawled into my tent to sleep but woke up several hours later with the awareness that something was wrong. I realized that Matt was no longer on the hill. Something had spooked him. Instead of being awakened by him, I found him sitting in a chair outside the sweatlodge.

During the closing sweat, the Spirits named him, Sky Dreamer. His vision quest was out of the ordinary, but then again, Matt always seemed to do things his own eccentric way.

Sky Dreamer's mother died two weeks later.

With sacred pipe in hand and his first vision quest under his belt, it was time for Matt to run sweatlodges. Every pipe carrier should be able to conduct this ceremony in case the medicine person is absent and the community needs to sweat. Leading the inipi was difficult for him. Even though he knew the form of the sweatlodge, he could not remain grounded while leading it. He would space out, leaving the participants afraid of what might happen next. Sky Dreamer was a perfect name for him.

I decided to let time and age temper him before allowing him to run a sweat ceremony again. That would be the right thing for Matt and for the community.

Before long, Matt was leading a discussion group on Native American spirituality at his college and invited me to be a speaker. Young people were looking to him, hungry for his natural, earthy way of spirituality.

A couple years after his first attempts to run a sweatlodge, Sky Dreamer asked if he could build a sweatlodge. I told him that he could, but that he should sweat alone until the Spirits said that he was ready for a community. Priscilla and I were preparing for our summer migration to Michigan. We would sweat with him when we returned to Massachusetts. At that time I would get a clear idea of whether or not he was ready to have his own sweatlodge community. Matt agreed.

After we had returned to our Massachusetts home, I told Sky Dreamer to invite special friends to an inipi ceremony at his new lodge the following weekend. Priscilla and I would attend. We wondered what kind of a lodge he had built. We laughed together about whether or not he would have all the tools and equipment to run a sweat, and we wondered how it would look. We expected the worse.

To our amazement, we saw a beautiful lodge. In spite of his frail body, he had leveled a good bit of land. The fire pit was perfectly placed. The whole location of the lodge and its construction were perfect. Priscilla kept the door from the outside, as the participants followed Sky Dreamer into this beautiful, sacred little structure.

Priscilla carried the red-hot stones to the door and Matt placed them carefully in the shallow pit with the confidence of someone who had been doing this for years. As the door was shut, he began a very powerful, spiritual ceremony. I grew in awe of the strength and newfound maturity of this young man. He had finally gotten grounded. A rather scary situation developed in the lodge as one of the participants experienced an emotional catharsis. Sky Dreamer reached deep into his intuition and handled the situation like a pro. Sky Dreamer had come into his own.

Throughout the fall, winter and spring, Matt developed his own sweatlodge community. He also continued to sweat with us when possible. I was peripherally aware that more and more young people were gathering around him, but he did not talk about that. We continued to meet together focused on his personal spiritual journey.

The following May, Priscilla and I once again prepared for our migration to Michigan. The early summer slipped by uneventfully until that fateful June when our daughter, Atsila Gaia, had her automobile accident in South Dakota. She spent the remainder of the summer with us, in daily rehab work, focusing on recovery. As the three of us were driving back to Massachusetts in mid-September, I received an urgent cell-phone message that Matt had been in a terrible accident while on vacation in California.

Sky Dreamer had flown to southern California with a friend. He was standing in the surf when a rogue wave smashed him to the sand. He suffered a high neck break which immediately rendered him a quadriplegic. As soon as we got home, I grabbed a flight to the west coast to join Matt's father and brother at his bedside.

It was awful. He was totally paralyzed and required a ventilator to breathe. An orthopedic surgeon operated to stabilize his neck. Sky Dreamer could not speak, but could only lip-sync words thus limiting our conversations.

Sky Dreamer needed to return to Massachusetts to be close to family and friends. The insurance company refused to cover the medical flight. No way could his family afford to fly him on a medical transport plane with specialists aboard to take care of him. Fortunately, Matt's brother had a connection in the governor's office. A call from that person helped the insurance company to discover that, indeed, the med flight was covered by his policy.

Unfortunately, before he left California, Matt's neck incision had become infected. Once settled into Boston Medical Center, all attention was focused on his hospital infection. It would get better. Then, it would get worse. Nothing seemed to stop it. Finally, it became clear to the medical staff that it wasn't going to be controlled. Matt would ultimately die from the infection eating away at his bones. Fortunately, Matt could feel no pain.

Sky Dreamer wanted so much to get well. He was willing to try anything, gene therapy, food supplements, anything. Soon, it became clear to him and to others that he would not survive the infection. His only control was the decision to determine the means and date of his own death, or to submit to the ravaging deterioration of his body in a nursing home.

I visited him every day. There were always young people there taking care of him, reading his lips and talking with him. Sometimes the room would be overflowing. Amazing! Here he was, unable to speak, but communicating with his eyes, his lips, and his wonderful smile. There were always one or two lovely young ladies tending to him, while the guys just "hung out."

He let his doctors know that he wanted to turn off his ventilator. They were willing to do that, but only after he went through psychiatric consults to be sure of his decision. Sky Dreamer told me he was thinking about doing it on a Thursday in a couple of weeks. He wanted Priscilla and me to sing him across with the native prayer songs. I told him that the day he had chosen wouldn't work for me. I had a dental appointment. Then he mentioned a couple of others. I knew he wasn't ready yet so I kept telling him that those days wouldn't work either. I said, "Matt. This is surreal. You aren't ready to make this decision yet." Priscilla told him that when his deceased mother came for him, he would know it was time to go.

Finally, one morning he said, "I want it turned off today." The staff was notified. There was a lot of necessary preparation. Family had to be called. The psychiatrist had to agree that he was ready. As we waited for the arrangements to be completed, a social worker confided to Priscilla that Matt told her he had been walking in the garden with his mother.

By 6:30 pm his wonderful Irish Catholic family had arrived. They loved Matt but didn't have a clue about his Native religion. However, they didn't seem to have a problem about the native way of helping him cross over.

When everything was ready, Priscilla and I began to sing the Lakota prayer songs. Matt was very quiet and composed as the ventilator was turned off. He looked toward Priscilla who was standing at the end of his bed. She smiled and gave him the "ones up" sign. As he began to gasp for air, the physician gave him a morphine shot to ease his discomfort, and Matt soared free from his broken body.

I hesitated a moment trying to decide which song to sing next, and his family broke in with the "The Lord's Prayer" followed by the "Hail Mary full of Grace." Knowing those prayers, I joined in and then returned to singing our prayer songs. It was a poignant time for everyone.

The family asked me to conduct his funeral. For the wake, Matt had told us that he wanted to be laid out on a lawn chair, wearing his beat-up jeans, his tie dye T shirt, Ray Ban sun glasses, his prayer bundle by his side, and a can of beer in his hand. I told him that I thought we could do everything except the lawn chair. Everyone who filed by the open casket had to smile at Matt's last request.

I arrived for the funeral a half hour ahead of time to be sure everything was arranged. There was no place to park. The funeral home parking lot was packed as were all the nearby streets. Amazed, I finally slipped into a "no parking" spot beside the mortuary. Inside, some 700 people had gathered to say good-bye to a beloved friend and teacher.

Jammed into every space in the funeral home, every room packed, was the most bizarre assortment of humanity imaginable. There were hippies loaded with tattoos, body piercing, jewels and spiked hair. There were bikers and their "chicks." There were well-dressed Catholic family members. It was overwhelming.

In his last days at Boston Hospital, Matt had asked me to run a memorial sweat ceremony for him at his own lodge. He promised he would attend.

Having promised Matt a memorial sweatlodge, we organized one for the following week. It would be in his home lodge and his friends and family were invited. As the time approached, we were filled with excitement and apprehension. It would be so good to see him and know that he was getting settled on the "other side," but we also wondered that he might be so occupied in his new world that he might not show up.

When the evening arrived, we filed into the sweatlodge. It wasn't long before we knew that Matt had also arrived. One of the nicest occurrences happened when Matt showed one of his favorite tie-died shirts. Suddenly, Matt's father saw his son's favorite tie-dye covering the far wall of the sweatlodge. Of course, it was pitch black in there but he clearly saw it. It meant so much to his father who had never been in a sweatlodge but had always supported Matt in his inipi work. It was a perfect gift from a loving son to his father.

A week later, Priscilla held a memorial sweatlodge ceremony in our home lodge because all of us felt like family with Matt. Again, he showed himself in the ceremony and was giddy happy. He was not only freed from his body, he was thoroughly enjoying everyone's reaction to his death and funeral. Priscilla told him that she was no longer going to grieve for him. How could she still mourn when he was so joyful. Priscilla told him that he needed to let go of this dimension and go on with the journey over there. He said his mother was right there with him saying the same thing.

Three years later, Priscilla and Atsila Gaia were hiking over a dam in Sky Dreamer's home town. There is a concrete structure on the dam housing machinery for controlling the water level. Painted on the concrete was, "He partied when he could, and he partied when he couldn't. We miss you, Matt."

Sky Dreamer was well loved. In his short life he had affected many people . . . including me.

CHAPTER **6**

OTTER HEART - SPIRIT SINGER

Loralee Dubeau (Otterheart) heard about our sweatlodge. We had been holding ceremony for several years and weren't looking for new members. However, a friend who was interested in Native American practices told me about her. She seemed like an individual who would provide even more depth to our community, so I offered her an invitation to participate in one of our inipi ceremonies. It was obvious that Loralee had a great deal of experience around ceremony. She had been a sacred pipe carrier for a couple of years.

Not only was she comfortable around the sweatlodge, she had also supported sundance, first at the Lonestar sundance and later at sundances with Mary Thunder. All these were authentic dances that took place in Texas.

She was not a person to draw attention to herself. She worked in the kitchen preparing food for the dancers and officials including the famous Lakota medicine man, Leonard Crow Dog. This was high-pressure work. People had to be fed on time. Everyone was incredibly busy. There was no time for ego or laziness. Like a traditional Indian woman, she was very humble. She told me about the sundances, but I don't think she mentioned them to our community unless asked about it. She was called Otterheart at that time.

Humility can also hide a very strong will. When needed, Otterheart could be tough. For instance, we had become lax in the sweat ceremony and sometimes would lapse into conversation as the sacred pipe was being smoked. It was hard for her. She was in tears when she admonished me about our lack of reverence in the presence of the pipe. Her daring to confront the Grandfather turned off some of our people. Actually, she was right, and I was appreciative and touched by her honesty.

Life had not been easy for her. She was born into a practicing Roman Catholic family. From early childhood she had been open to the Spirit world. She saw people who had crossed over. She heard them. When a grandparent died, she told her parents before relatives called with the sad news.

Most troubling for her parents, were her mentions of visitations by beings from other worlds. Having been squashed so often by adults in her world, it is only in the last few years that she has been willing to talk about these things.

You can imagine the difficulties this strange daughter caused her parents. To them, their child almost seemed to be possessed by some evil force. Good Catholic children did not talk about seeing ghosts. Her mother begged her to keep quiet. Otherwise, she might be "hospitalized."

When she went to Catholic school, the nuns were even more taken aback by this weird child. She would often answer questions before they were asked. She mentioned her psychic experiences. Of course, they did not seem psychic to her. It was all natural. However, she soon learned to hold her tongue about such things.

As an adult, she did psychic readings for people. She studied the arts of Cartomancy (card reading) and Astrology and used them, augmented by her strong intuitive awareness. As a young adult she was called by her Native Spirits to recognize her distant Indian lineage. She did it with great energy and dedication. She had been part of a sweatlodge community in western Massachusetts for a few years followed by a short time in a community in Connecticut. Ultimately, she was guided to us.

Her adult life was also tough. She taught spiritual and native subjects evenings in a couple of community colleges. She regularly provided medicine wheel ceremonies at a nearby buffalo farm. She spent seventeen years working in a filter/optic factory where the atmosphere was heavy with chemical fumes. There were weekends when her lungs were very irritated during our sweatlodge ceremonies, but she never stopped coming. Over the years, this constant chemical onslaught took a toll on her body.

It was about two weeks before Priscilla and I planned to make our migration to Priscilla's ancestral home in Michigan that we were out hiking with our dogs when suddenly, Grandfather Ishnala Mani (my primary Spirit Teacher) said, "Sweat Otterheart before you go."

I said, "Grandfather, I don't have time to do that. We are down to the last days before our move. I have too much to do. I don't have a day to make a fire and prepare a lodge."

He replied simply, "Sweat Otterheart before you go."

"Grandfather, please, I don't have time."

"Sweat Otterheart before you go."

"Okay."

When we got home I phoned her with the news that we had to sweat, just the two of us, in the next few days. Of course, she wanted to know why we needed to sweat. I told her simply that Grandfather demanded it.

She agreed. A few days later we prepared a sweatlodge. At the appropriate time in the sweat, I asked, "Grandfather, what is this all about?"

He said, "She is to be your successor. Teach her everything you know."

This was scary as I wasn't ready to depart this world. He assured me that it wasn't about my dying. They had other plans for me.

Just because the Spirits ask you do something, you always have a choice to agree or refuse. After a couple of days, Otterheart called to say that she was willing, so we both accepted the Spirits' request. I was teacher for the whole sweatlodge community, but now I would also be teaching Otterheart the things she would need as a sacred person, one who would lead sweatlodge communities.

It was clear that she needed a mate who would stand by her, honor her uniqueness, and help her live a more healthy life. Her prayers were answered when a man attending one of her classes asked her for a date. It wasn't long before I had the honor of marrying them in a traditional ceremony.

As she grew in her leadership role, the time came for our camp to divide, with part of the group following her to an inipi community she was establishing. It was a time of grateful tears as well as celebration. Separation is always difficult and we were a very close family, but it was natural for Otterheart to establish herself as a Native sweatlodge leader.

I suggested that she seek initiation into the Good Medicine Society, a group dedicated to teaching medicine ways. It had been founded by Old Settler Cherokees who migrated to the Ozark Mountains in Arkansas before the Trail of Tears in 1836. I had been associated with the society for many years. Grandmother Alloday, head of the society, welcomed her with open arms, and Otterheart completed her initial studies quickly. She progressed in her training until she is now an Elder teacher in the society.

Although no longer sharing in ceremony, we remained close, and I continued to be her teacher but felt that I had given her what I knew.

In early 2012 she was sitting in her meditation room having conference with a group of Spirit Grandmothers when my late teacher, George Whitewolf, interrupted. He dismissed all the Grandmothers and proceeded to remonstrate with Otterheart that she had not finished her studies with me.

She answered, "But Grandfather tells me he has taught me everything and that we are finished."

Whitewolf answered, "No. You have to pester him the same way he pestered me. There is something yet to do."

It turned out that I had not publicly acknowledged that she was to be a successor of mine. After a series of sacred pipe and sweat-lodge ceremonies, the Spirits said that we were complete. In a special chanupa ceremony, they gave her a new name, Spirit Singer, which recognizes both her relationships to the Spirits and to her being part of the Sings-Alone spiritual family. This was followed by a public ceremony with many family and friends in attendance and where I acknowledged her for the whole world.

The reader may be puzzled by the above episode. While it is not an everyday occurrence, Spirit communication is perfectly normal in the Indian world and among medicine people.

Priscilla asked Spirit Singer when she planned to write the book about her experiences. She was surprised because she hadn't told anyone that the Spirits had told her to write a book. She struggled with it and finally wrote, *There's A Whole In The Sky* (by Loralee Dubeau), as a fictional novel. But we all know that sometimes fiction allows us to get at a greater truth than does a biography.

PART 2

RED PATH ZEN: HONORING THE LINEAGES

What an honor for me to hold two great lineages: Zen Buddhism and Lakota Spirituality. We know so much more about the Zen lineage because there are written documents going back 2000 years. We honor the names of 89 ancestors who were major teachers in each generation. How I wish we knew the names of Lakota teachers back through the years. We can only go back several generations. It is fascinating, however, that both spiritual traditions stress the importance of honoring the line of ancestral teachers.

CHAPTER 7

LINEAGE OF CHIEF FRANK FOOLS CROW

Fools Crow is the nominal head of my Native lineage although he learned from Black Elk, Stirrup and probably others. Most of us look back to Fools Crow because we were honored to know him in person. I began to walk the Red Road in 1973 just after the Wounded Knee fiasco. Fools Crow didn't die until 1989 so our lives overlapped a little.

It boggles the mind to think that Fools Crow was two generations away from the Stone Age. He was born, we think, in 1890, and lived through the end of the war with the US government and the restriction of the plains Indians to reservations. His grandparents were a migratory people, following the herds of buffalo, dragging tipi poles upon which were bound their few necessary possessions. They did not have the wheel. They did not use metal until traders introduced it. However, they were expert horsemen.

The government paid hunters to slaughter the great buffalo herds so that the native people would be starved into submission. By Fools Crow's birth, the herds were gone. He did not see a live buffalo until he was a teenager on a train trip. They passed a farm where the white owner had a small herd. Fools Crow saw the man hand-feeding them, and was amazed at the sight. For him the buffalo was a mythic figure, fierce and untamable. Here was a white man, so powerful that he could hand-feed the great beast.

A very holy medicine man, Stirrup, had been watching the boy, Fools Crow, and saw that he had the potential to become a spiritual leader. When Fools Crow was thirteen years old, Stirrup conducted him on a vision quest.

There are several ways to experience a vision quest. Typically, one is placed within an altar area, enclosed by tobacco ties. One stays there for a predetermined time, one to four days, without food, water, or shelter, dressed only in a towel or simple cotton shift, and with a blanket for cover. A purifying sweatlodge is given before ascending the hill, and immediately upon coming down. In the final lodge, the person relates all visions and experiences to the medicine man who then inquires of the Spirits the meaning of those experiences and events.

A more physically rigorous vision quest may be experienced in a grave-sized pit. This is where thirteen-years-old Fools Crow was placed. The pit, six feet long by three feet wide by four feet deep had been dug. The bottom was covered with purifying sage. Fools Crow jumped into the pit to lie, watch, and wait for four days. He wore a simple breach clout and had only a blanket with him. A buffalo hide was pegged securely over the pit leaving him in complete darkness. We don't know what he experienced, but Fools Crow told author Thomas Mails that his visions at that tender age were life-transforming.

Stirrup continued to be his basic teacher for the medicine road. Fools Crow also spent a great deal of time with his uncle, Black Elk, a widely respected medicine man. Over the course of his lifetime, Fools Crow was honored as a healer, teacher and ceremonial chief of the Oglala Lakota nation. He lived to be a hundred years old, dying in 1989. He was, I think, 94 when I saw him the last time as he conducted the first east coast sundance for the Piscataway Nation in Maryland.

Grandfather Fools Crow became the teacher of my teacher, George Whitewolf.

Whitewolf had been very involved in the American Indian Movement's struggle to protect the rights and sovereignty of the Native Tribes. During this time he experienced his first sweatlodge. Up to that point, his small farm had been the scene of Indian weekend pow-wows and parties with lots of drinking and excess. After his introduction into the Native Spiritual life, he stopped the drunken bashes, and his home became a sweatlodge community.

Whitewolf joined a group of young men who were learning from Grandpa Fools Crow. He was very proud of that relationship and loved to show a pair of beaded moccasins that Grandma Fools Crow made for him. Whitewolf was an avid student. Before long he became a pipe carrier and had his own sweatlodge community. Eventually he became known as a Wicasa Wakan (holy man).

Time passed. Fools Crow felt his powers waning with age. He sent Whitewolf to learn from Dawson No Horse. No Horse was a nephew of Fools Crow and was recognized as a powerful medicine man, arguably the most powerful of his generation.

No Horse is especially interesting as he was a Lay Reader in the Pine Ridge Episcopal Church, the largest Lakota Speaking Church on the reservation. The Rev. Paul Steinmetz in his book, *Pipe, Bible and Peyote among the Oglala Lakota,* said that Dawson No Horse first came to the sacred pipe through a gallstone healing by Chief Fools Crow.

Whitewolf, however, told me a very different story. The sundance was about to be performed on Pine Ridge. At this point, the people called No Horse a Reverend even though he was only a Lay Reader. He had nothing to do with Lakota religion and thought of it as superstition. He was taken aback when a nephew called and said, "Uncle, I am going to dance in the sun dance. I want you to come and support me."

No Horse knew about the sundance ceremony even though he never participated in one. He knew that as the dancers moved back and forth in front of the cottonwood tree, a large number of friends and family would gather under arbors surrounding the dance arena. While the sundancers moved inside the arena, their supporters on the outside would be swaying in sync with them. Just by attending, he would become part of the ceremony which for four days would begin soon after sunrise and continue to sunset with periodic breaks during the day.

Dawson had no intention of wasting his time on sundances. "Nephew, you know that I don't have anything to do with those old superstitions."

"I know, Uncle, but I really want you there."

No matter how strongly he argued, his nephew was adamant. The obligations of blood relationship overwhelmed Dawson's reservations, and he agreed to attend.

His idea was to slip in behind the crowd and try to be invisible. With everyone knowing him as Rev. No Horse, he didn't want anyone to think he approved of this pagan nonsense.

The opening day of Sun Dance arrived and No Horse assumed his place, being as inconspicuous as possible. Frank Fools Crow stepped to the microphone to begin the dance. Looking out over the crowd, he paused, and then said, "I see we have Rev. No Horse with us. Dawson, would you come over here and give an invocation for us?"

No Horse nearly fainted. His cover blown, he edged out of the crowd and started across the dance arena to the announcer's booth. Everyone watched with fascination as the Reverend, who had been so opposed to traditional spirituality, moved toward Fools Crow.

Dawson suddenly stopped, facing the sun dance tree, his face transfixed. All eyes were on him and everyone knew something was happening.

As it was told later, Dawson saw Jesus step out of the tree. He spoke to Dawson, "I need you to follow the ways of your people. Your people need you. I want you to do this."

From that day, guided by Fools Crow, Dawson became a Wicasa Wakan, a Holy man, and a great spiritual teacher for the people. Whitewolf was one of many young men in Dawson's camp.

So my Native lineage is from Whitewolf to No Horse to Fools Crow to Stirrup and Black Elk, back into the shadows of sacred history.

CHAPTER 8

SHAKYAMUNI BUDDHA

Buddhism takes many forms, and has spread around the world from India, the Near and Far East to North and South America, Europe, Australia, and New Zealand. Zen Buddhism is among the largest and in some ways the most simple and fundamental form, but all Buddhists honor and recognize Siddhartha Gautama of the Shakya clan. After his enlightenment when he began teaching, he was sometimes known as Shakyamuni, the Sage (muni) of the Shakyas. His most formal title is Shakyamuni Buddha. Buddha means Awakened One.

He was once asked if he was a god. He said, "No. I am a man who has awakened." Buddhism is based on the Dharma, teachings that the Buddha has uncovered in his efforts to become enlightened and what he discovered from his awakening. These teachings guide us in our own personal efforts to awaken, and encourage us to care for the well-being and harmony of all creation. In the words of Roshi Genki, "We care for all creation because it is our Self," and we attempt to live by those teachings.

Zen Buddhism is not founded on a divine person, a God, as is Christianity. Christianity is based on belief in the divinity of Christ. According to Buddhist tradition, there have been six ages prior to the current one. In each age a Buddha uncovered the Dharma for that time. So, our Shakyamuni Buddha has uncovered the Dharma for us, and we continue that teaching. While not a God, he is a deeply revered figure and the founder of all Buddhism.

We look back 2500 years to a small "kingdom" somewhere near Nepal. There are several myths describing the place and circumstances of his birth. The most common story claims he was born in Lumbini, Nepal. There are other contenders for his birthplace. We will never know for sure. There is also no agreement among scholars as to his exact birth date. Some place it at 563 B.C.E. and others as late as 400 B.C.E.

Tradition says that he was born into a royal Hindu family. His father was king Suddhodana of the Shakyatriya clan. His mother died soon after he was born. He was raised by an aunt. The King determined to protect his son from the ugliness of harsh reality. Seers, at the time of Buddha's birth, foretold that he would become either a great king or a great holy man. The King, of course, wanted his son to choose the Royal role, and had his son raised in all manner of king craft and warfare.

Shakyamuni (Sage of the Shakyas) was married at 16 to a cousin of the same age. Together they had a son and lived in great luxury. Shakyamuni was trained to be a warrior king, but his father had protected him from seeing the outside world with all its pain and sadness. It would seem a contradiction to want your son to be a hardened military leader, but protect him from exposure to the tough side of life. Nevertheless, when it was necessary to travel outside the royal compounds, the king would have the village area and streets cleared so that his son would be spared seeing the awfulness that could often be found there.

At age 29, Shakyamuni wanted to see the unadorned kingdom. He was no longer willing to live in such a closed environment. He wanted to see the people he would someday rule. His charioteer probably argued strongly against the idea, but ultimately agreed to help the

Buddha escape the family compound and venture into the surrounding city. In the dark of night, Shakyamuni and his driver slipped out of the stables and headed into the city. There the Buddha was aghast upon encountering people who were in pain, sick and old. He saw decaying corpses and confronted the face of death for the first time. The sights were overwhelming. It didn't take long before he was ready to retreat to the loveliness of his home and his young wife.

He couldn't get the awful sights out of his mind. He had never seen skeletal people dying of hunger or the stooped bodies of the aged. There was a smell to sickness and certainly to death. Life that he never imagined was happening all around him. Misery surrounded the opulence of the royal compounds. His people were not happy. They were sick, hungry, diseased, poorly dressed, and death was an ever threatening presence. His concept of the meaning of life was shaken to the core. There had to be more to life than such awful suffering on one hand and enormous luxury on the other.

He became restless and slipped away into the city several more times. On one journey he came upon a Sadhu, a holy man, meditating. In questioning his charioteer, he learned that such renunciates were searching to transcend ordinary misery and find a deeper meaning and relation to life. It was believed that such men might escape the cares and burdens of human beings by attaining spiritual maturity and unity with the Sacred. It was a life style that many believed in but few attempted.

One night, he and his charioteer once again slipped out of the compound. Shakyamuni shucked off his royal garb and wrapped himself in the loin cloth of a begging ascetic. What an abrupt and drastic change in life for him! Here was a young man used to luxury and comfort, suddenly shedding everything upon which he once relied. Now, he had nothing. . . no food, no clothes, no shelter. He was on the quest. I am not sure he knew what he was seeking, but he took the most radical form of quest that was available to him.

At first he followed two of the most famous teachers of his time, and quickly mastered all they had to offer. At the summit of their teachings, however, he found himself not satisfied, still locked in the cycle of birth and death, still on the wheel of becoming. Then, he took an even more radical form of quest available to him. Determined to eradicate the self, tradition says he ate only one grain of rice a day. Finally, nearing death from starvation, he was saved by the kindness of a young woman who seeing this near corpse of a man, tenderly persuaded him to take some cow's milk and rice.

Shakyamuni discovered that starvation was not the path to liberation. Thus, he renounced extreme asceticism and began to practice a middle way, somewhere between self-indulgence and self-denial. Still, he could not satisfy the spiritual hunger that tormented him. A fulfilling connection with the sacred hovered just out of reach.

Finally, Shakyamuni planted himself beneath the Bodhi tree and announced he would sit there until he found enlightenment. He sat in meditation for forty-nine days until he experienced the "Ah hah" moment when the confusion in his mind evaporated, and he was filled with understanding. At age thirty-five he became the Buddha, the enlightened one. He saw a basic truth that all life is suffering caused by false desires and attachments – wanting what isn't, not wanting what is.

There is much more to suffering than just pain, hunger and death. Suffering may come from greed, from anger, from addiction, from hunger, from fear of dying, from constantly wanting more than what you have. There are many causes for the gnawing that human beings feel in their deep consciousness. From his experience and realization, he formulated the Four Noble Truths and the Eight Fold Path:

Four Noble Truths

1. Suffering exists

2. Suffering arises from attachment to desires

3. Suffering ceases when attachment to desire ceases

4. Freedom from suffering is possible by practicing the Eightfold Path

Noble Eightfold Path

	Eightfold Path
Wisdom *(panna)*	Right View
	Right Thought
Morality *(sila)*	Right Speech
	Right Action
	Right Livelihood
Meditation *(samadhi)*	Right Effort
	Right Mindfulness
	Right Contemplation

Soon, followers gathered around him. In the course of time he accepted the vows of poverty and practice from both men and women, and ordained many monks and nuns who shaved their heads, donned rag robes dyed with saffron and followed him everywhere imitating his homeless lifestyle. For forty-five years he taught whomever would listen, farmers and merchants, monks and nuns, and even kings.

Shakyamuni Buddha lived a most simple life. He had no dwelling and wandered from place to place. He begged food and spent hours every day in meditation. He daily taught in public assembly. Numbering in the thousands, his followers memorized his words which were later assembled in written collections, the earliest about 400 years after his death.

The Buddha died at age 80 after a life of teaching the Dharma. He taught a radical concept of liberation. Truth would not be found by logical discourse. It would be found by a deep existential immersion in the awareness of Oneness; not by retreating into meditative absorption, nor by insisting that every creation is an homogenized whole, but by seeing and being with things "as they truly are." Sometimes the simplest teaching can produce the most profound results.

After Shakyamuni Buddha many female and male master teachers carried on his work, men like Bodhi Dharma who carried Buddhism from India to China, Dogen who left his home in Japan to study in China and then brought the teachings back to Japan. In our time, folks such as Shunryu Suzuki Roshi and Taizan Maezumi Roshi among others imported Zen Buddhism from Japan to the western world. Eighty-nine illustrious names grace my personal lineage all the way back to Shakyamuni Buddha. I am a priest and Dharma Successor to Roshi Paul Genki Kahn within the Zen Garland Order.

One of the key ways that Zen and Native American teachings are similar is that both emphasize the Oneness of all things, and that the basic teachings are transmitted in personal relationship from teacher to student down through the ages. Such different cultures with such similar concepts bear witness to the unity of sacred understanding. I proudly hold both lineages. Red Path Zen represents two separate practice paths integrated in a compatible and powerful unity of purpose. Who knows what the future holds? But for now, I am committed to this new/old way, fully Zen and authentically Native American..

CHAPTER 9

FINDING ZEN

How is it that someone who has so devotedly followed the Red Road for forty years suddenly becomes a Zen Buddhist? It is a legitimate question. I never dreamed that I might someday be a Zen Priest and Sensei.

In my first book, *Sprinting Backwards to God,* I described my ill-fated journey into the Protestant ministry. When it finally became impossible to ignore the Spirits' multiple warnings that this was not my path, I was lost in a spiritual vacuum having no religious base or identity. There were evenings I would sit in front of the statue of the Blessed Virgin in our university Catholic parish and just cry from my empty heart.

On one of those nights, I had a power dream. I rarely have these, but when they come, I pay attention. This was true even before I followed the Red Road. In this dream I was taken in a small motorboat off the coast of Florida. A man was at the wheel. A woman sat beside me. I did not know her nor did I have a name for her. Puzzled by what was happening, I kept quiet, paying attention.

In time a mountainous island appeared on the horizon. As we drew closer, I saw temples of various types shrouded among the trees. There was an ancient Greek temple. There was some kind of Christian structure, perhaps a monastery, and there were other sacred temples.

However, down front, dominating the scene, was a huge Buddha statue sitting in meditation.

I was immediately drawn to Him. The boat, however, did not stop at the front of the island, but rather began to motor to the back side where there was a rickety old dock. I was told to disembark, but I had the distinct impression that I could not go directly to the Buddha or any of the temples.

At that point I stumbled upon a group of men in some kind of a ceremony by a sacred fire. I understood somehow that this would become my home. I belonged to the fire. However, I never forgot the Buddha sitting there, actively waiting. Upon awakening the next morning, I drew a picture of the mountain and the Buddha. I kept that drawing, intuitively knowing it offered a key to my spiritual journey.

For the next couple of years, I read all the popular books about Hinduism and Buddhism, books like *Be Here Now* by Ram Das, and although I spent the 1950's in college and seminary, I returned to grad school in 1966. Like so many others in that period, I patiently turned Ram Das's book like a wheel, following its crazy outlay, trying to understand the spiritual basis of what I was seeking.

Baba Muktananda, one of the traveling Indian Gurus, had an ashram near the University of Florida where I was first in the doctoral program, then a teaching assistant, and later, an assistant professor. There was incredible excitement when the announcement appeared that Babaji was coming to Gainesville. Some of my students who thought of me as a kind of New Age teacher, asked if I could set them up for a satsang (teaching) with him. Knowing some of his people, I was able to arrange for us to attend a morning satsang along with about one hundred other people.

On the appointed day we showed up and joined the crowd sitting cross-legged on the floor waiting for Muktananda to arrive. After a suitable time, he came and settled onto a special safron throne raised above floor level. Devotees approached him on their knees, bringing offerings of fruit.

I had read some of his teachings in preparation for the satsang. I wanted to have at least an idea of his beliefs. As best I could understand, he taught that if one wants to find God, one does not seek Him in a teacher, but finds God or Shiva in one's own heart. I thoroughly enjoyed this little old man who sat on his safron throne, receiving homage while his eyes twinkled. I thought he was laughing inwardly at people who were unable or unwilling to find God within, but sought Him in a Guru.

After a brief teaching, translated by his assistant, Muktananda whispered something in his helper's ear. The assistant came down to me and said "Babaji wants you to come to him." I did not know what to do at this point. I wasn't about to go crawling to him, but wanting to be respectful, I approached him while bowing deeply. He reached up, pulled me into his arms. I found myself, twice his size and height, cuddled in his lap. His assistant whispered in my ear, "Babaji says you don't need to go to satsangs. You have the Shakti moving in you already."

I was, of course, aware that my stock was rapidly rising in the eyes of my students who were seeing me in a new light, but I had no idea what all this meant. Later, Muktananda invited me to join his followers in a weekend retreat.

I found myself the next morning at 4:00 AM rising, washing my face, and entering a large concrete floored room, already filled by his many followers sitting in meditation. I settled in, not knowing how to meditate, crossed my legs and waited. . . for half an hour. . .for an hour. By this point my ankles were killing me from resting on hard concrete. Without a pillow or a zafu, my knees were complaining. I decided that although I liked the ego boost of having the Shakti and all that, this wasn't my path. I got up and left.

Some of my students gave me a single peacock feather and half jokingly called me a "one feathered" guru. I spoke deep thoughts, shared profundities, and became an expert about things I did not understand. This common hubris was both the curse and blessing of the 70's. We were all searching for spirituality. Some of us thought we knew more than we did, victims of our egos.

Fortunately, within a couple of years I was saved by Rolling Thunder who firmly set my feet on the Red Road.

As mentioned earlier, after three years with Rolling Thunder and seven years with Whitewolf, training in native spirituality, and more than twenty years teaching the same, we left Maryland and moved to Massachusetts where we established a small, sweatlodge community dedicated to training a few participants to become pipe carriers and teachers. Among those who joined us was a young man and his girl-friend. He was, at that time, an active Zen Buddhist and student in the Zen Peace Maker seminary.

I had been practicing my own kind of meditation for some time but became interested in Zen as he described it. However, my total focus remained on teaching Native American concepts and offering sweatlodge and pipe ceremonies. This young man kept suggesting that I would enjoy meeting the spiritual director of the Zen Peacemakers, Roshi Paul Genki Kahn. I was interested but figured both the Roshi and I were too busy to take the time to get acquainted.

Then, one night after a routine but hot sweatlodge ceremony when I was deep in sleep, a voice pushed itself into my conscious-ness. "That was your last sweatlodge."

Groggily, I groaned, "Huh?"

"That was your last sweatlodge."

I heard my voice stammer, "Grandfather, I don't understand, but I am exhausted from the sweatlodge last night. I can't deal with this right now."

First thing next morning, I took my chanupa wakan (sacred pipe), went out to the sweatlodge, opened my bundle and begged for clarification.

"Hau, Grandfather, what do you want of me? The sweatlodge has been my spiritual home for thirty years. If I cannot sweat, what will I do?"

Depression and sadness began to overwhelm me, my portal to the sacred slamming in my face.

Then the Grandfather Spirit spoke, "As long as you are grounded in the sweatlodge you won't be doing what we need you to do. We want you to teach non-native people how to live together in mutual respect and Oneness. They must learn that their lives are totally entwined with the health of Grandmother Earth. They need to learn from you the ways of respect and being a hollow bone."

Now I began to understand why the Spirits chose Spirit Singer to be my first successor so that I could begin to focus on teaching outside the native community.

As noted by many natives and psychically aware people, a new age of heightened consciousness and awareness is dawning. People are beginning to remember what it means to be human beings . . . to love, respect, and care for each other and Grandmother Earth. But the old ways of selfishness, hatred, greed, and ignorance are still struggling to maintain their hold. Life is hard. Birth is always difficult and dangerous. The forces of the status quo fight against evolutionary change.

When the Grandfathers yanked me from the sweatlodge to reach out to non-natives, they tore the spiritual grounding out from under me. It took me a while to stop whining, although Priscilla says that I still have my moments.

"Grandfathers, what do I teach? What is appropriate to teach in the Anglo community? I can't teach the importance of the inipi, for that ceremony is seldom open to outsiders. I have no interest in urging non-Indians to go buy sacred pipes when they have no training for the respectful uses of the pipe. Most modern Anglo women are resentful when told that they must not participate in certain ceremonies, or handle the pipe when they are in their moontime (menstrual period). What do you want me to do?"

The Grandfathers answered, "Teach people how to live in harmony with themselves, with each other, and Grandmother Earth. People are out of balance. Human beings are moving into a time of crisis and earth changes. There will be much suffering. If they are to survive in a good way, they must learn how to nurture their own spirits, how to care for those in need whether human, animal or plant. Teach them to live in the spirit of Mitakuye Oyas'in (all my relations), to live in awareness of our Oneness with all creation. Teach them the true meaning of Walking in Beauty."

"Okay," I said, "But where do I teach?" I had tried already to offer Native Spirituality workshops in various venues with little success. I said, "I am willing to teach, but you have to open doors for me."

Then, I remembered that Roshi Genki and the Zen Peacemakers had been highly recommended to me. It turned out that the Roshi was interested in what I had to offer. Within a couple of weeks, at his invitation, I was presenting a workshop in the mother Zendo of the Zen Peacemaker Order. The workshop participants, including the Roshi and his assistant, were very impressive to me. They were respectful and interested in the Native Spiritual concepts. Since then, I have taught in many Zen venues.

When I first attended a Zen service, listening to the chants and the lovely resonance of the gong and the happy tingling of the bells, I felt I had come home to a place I had known forever. Perhaps that was true.

The Buddha on the mountain of my vision had called, and I heard Him after all these years. I could see right away that the Native approach and the Zen approach to life and Creation were very similar. Both traditions place humankind in direct relation to all creations. I make that word plural here, "creations," to emphasize each and everything, not just a vague totality. Native spirituality is focused on

Grandmother Earth in an ecological sensitivity that values the inter-dependence of each and every creature, plant, and mineral, as well as the planet. Interdependence is certainly a cornerstone of Zen en-lightenment, but perhaps Zen folks could learn how to step more lightly on the Grandmother. This is one of the gifts the Red Path brings to Zen.

CHAPTER 10

MAN PRAYER, WOMAN PRAYER, AND ZAZEN

The hub of Native Spirituality is the chanupa wakan (sacred pipe). I had flirted with various forms of meditation, but meditation proper began for me in settling myself down with the pipe.

Native tradition teaches two forms of prayer. Priscilla Cogan describes them as "man prayer" and "woman prayer." Although I never heard Whitewolf use those terms, they fit the teaching exactly.

Women and men use these forms alike. In man prayer, the pipe is pointed to the west and a request is made out loud. It is interesting to note that nearly all tribes face the east for prayers and ceremonies. Only the Oglala Lakota face the west. I was trained by the Oglala, so I am a west-facing ceremonialist. During prayers, requests may be for oneself, for another, or for anything. It is the way one lays out an agenda of things for which one needs the help of the Grandfather and Grandmother Spirits.

Woman prayer is quite different. The pipe bowl is held in the left hand and the tip is pointed to the west (or east). If it is being held for a period of time during meditation, it may be leaned comfortably against ones chest. One empties oneself and becomes open and receptive. It is a time of waiting for guidance, for answers, even answers to questions not asked. Generally man prayer is done first. Putting ones questions and concerns out into the universe makes a space inside for answers during woman prayer.

Woman prayer roughly corresponds to the absorptive, concentrated form of Zen meditation (zazen). In Zen, this form cultivates Samadhi, a unitive state of consciousness which generates prana, chi or ki, and circulates this vital, healing energy throughout the body. Other forms of Zen meditation are quite different in practice and purpose, such as koan meditation and shikantaza (sitting in Presence).

Whitewolf was a bull in a china shop. I can hear him laughing now, "Duncan, for God's sake just shut up and pray. He was not one for abstract thought or theological nujances. He would never have been interested in Zen. From his point of view the world needs nothing more than a chanupa and inipi. The last words I ever heard from him were, "Duncan, you read too much. Stop buying so many books."

I respectfully disagree with him. The problem is that chanupa wakan (sacred pipe), the inipi (sweatlodge), and vision quest (hanblecheya), are not easily available or appropriate for the general public.

One has to also consider that the inipi and chanupa wakan are part of a larger cultural picture. The Lakota and other native people live embedded in nature. They know in their hearts that they are One with Grandmother Earth and all her children: animal, vegetable and mineral. Whenever in need, they can take out their pipes and pray. Sweatlodges are all around them on tribal lands.

Although they might not participate in an inipi ceremony regularly, Native Americans who are still living in their sacred traditions, live and breathe in a world of awareness, natural spirituality, and Oneness.

In the urban world, it is difficult to identify with nature where it is so often relegated to the periphery of awareness. When I was in New

York City, except for Central Park, trees were growing in little circles cut into the concrete as if nature is alien, something to be feared.

A lucky few non-Indians have been invited into a sweatlodge community where they come up close and personal with Grandmother Earth. In this face to face encounter with the Grandmother, they may experience a vivid and powerful spiritual event and know in their hearts that they are One with creation. But my concern is that an occasional sweatlodge experience, powerful as it may be, is not enough to produce lasting change and deepened spirituality. Nor is the sweatlodge available to most non-natives.

With Zen, the transformative ceremony is Zen meditation. People can meditate daily at home or a nearby Zendo. There are regular opportunities to meditate with others, so that a spiritual community with its grounding is available. It is my experience that Zen and Native American spirituality together can more effectively produce spiritual change in a way that periodic sweatlodges cannot. Red Path Zen brings the power to Zen of the Native American emphasis on how the interrelationship of all things needs to be respected and protected. Red Path Zen affords a powerful, unitive, life changing experience that is seldom found in our technological society.

Meditation has always been important to me even though earlier I practiced forms other than zazen, Zen type meditation. I had been wanting to host a meditation group of my neighbors to create a sense of community and deepened spirituality in my neighborhood. The local newspaper printed a small announcement that a meditation group was forming, and within a week some twenty-six people, none of whom were Indian or Buddhists, called to inquire. As I became more involved in Zen, the group evolved into a Zen Sangha, a Buddhist practicing community.

From my early adulthood I have always been a priest/teacher, so it was within my natural evolution to take the vows and precepts and be ordained as a Zen Buddhist priest. Later, after extended study and reading of the classics, I was empowered as a Dharma Successor to Roshi Paul Genki Kahn. Today I am a proud Soto Zen Priest and Sensei in the Zen Garland Order. I stand in two powerful lineages . . . my Native American lineage from Buffalo Calf Woman through Grandfather Fools Crow on down through George Whitewolf to me, and from Shakyamuni Buddha through Roshi Genki to me. I love my sacred pipe and my heart sings with the sound of the Zen gong and chants. I am doing exactly what the Grandfathers asked of me. I am blessed.

Roshi Genki asked me to develop a Native American Zen path within the Zen Garland Order. Red Path Zen is now a growing practice path for those who want to enrich their spirituality with Native and Zen concepts and practices.

The following pages will explain what it means to walk the Red Path in Zen, which is fully Zen and authentically native American.

CHAPTER 11

DEEP SPIRITUALITY THE RED PATH ZEN WAY

What are the first steps in practicing Red Path Zen?

The very first thing is to take time to be silent. We can't live every waking hour at a breakneck pace, gobbling information from our multiple cyber portals to the universe, then spend an hour in church on Sunday, an evening in a Zen Sangha, or several hours around an occasional inipi ceremony on Saturday and expect to grow very much in Spirit. Most people feel a need to fill every available moment with frenetic activity or with passive entertainment in front of the TV. There is nothing especially wrong with this, but it probably won't satisfy the spiritual hunger you may feel.

If you want to develop a spiritual life, you must make time for it. Let me say this again. If you want to develop a spiritual life, you must make time for it. As a young college graduate, I entered seminary to become a Protestant minister. I was immediately sent to an internship parish where I could practice what I was learning in class. What with commuting to school every day, taking classes, studying, and ministering to my church members, I had no time to pray or meditate. My parsonage was fifty miles from seminary, and my first class was at 7:00 AM. There was no thought given to this by the faculty. The students were so busy learning the tools of their trade that they had no time to relate to God by whatever name. It was assumed that the students were already spiritual or they wouldn't be in the seminary. Spirituality, however, does not grow that way.

Every day, make time to sit in quietness. This does not mean to kneel in prayer for a few moments. Most prayer, as mentioned earlier, is what we call "man prayer" where you lay out an agenda to God.

"Please do this. . . Please do that." This type of beseeching prayer is typical in church services. But I think that the more important form of prayer is "Woman Prayer" in which one sits quietly, opens the heart, and pays attention, waiting for the Spirit to speak. Most of the time with "Man Prayer" we state our needs and desires, say "Amen," and return to our busyness. We would be frightened out of our wits if anyone immediately responded or anything happened. Most people pray with their eyes closed. If a Grandfather or Grandmother Spirit appeared and had anything to say in response to their prayers, they wouldn't see Him or Her.

Effective man prayer requires clear intent and visualization. For instance, if you are praying that someone be healed, it is important to be very clear that this is a priority for you, and you have no internal vacillation about it. The next thing is very important. Visualize, see in your imagination the individual getting out of bed, smiling, being strong. When you can see it in your mind's eye, you are putting that prayer, that energy, out into the ether, and it carries healing power. If you pray for someone who is ill, and you see him only as sick or dying, then your prayer is "Let this person be sick and let them die." It is important that you visualize what you really want to have happen. If there is any secret or magic in prayer, it is visualization. So, man prayer is a very important and necessary part of one's spirituality.

It is interesting that when you express your prayers with clear intention, their power travels in two directions. It extends into the universe, but it also opens a space in your own heart for an answer.

In "Woman Prayer" sit quietly, keep your eyes open, pay attention to everything and *expect* something to happen. We have a tradition of vision quest (hanblecheya) in which an individual goes "on the hill" to pray from one to four days without food, water, shelter, or the sight of another human. It takes all of thirty minutes to complete all the man prayers one desires to make. The rest of the time is spent in watching and waiting and being open to the Spirits.

One young woman went on hanblecheya (vision quest) for a day and night. In the inipi, alone with the medicine man, she was asked to reiterate what had happened.

She was silent.

The medicine man asked, "Did anything happen up there?"

She said, "no."

"Did you see anything, or did anything come to you?"

"No."

"What did you pray for?" he asked, puzzled.

"I was afraid, so I prayed that nothing would happen."

A funny and true story, but her fears simply mirror the ambivalent fear of many people, afraid that no one will hear their prayers, afraid that someone will answer!

Now if the vision quester does not hush and pay attention, he or she may well miss something important. The least one can do, is to be open to the possibility that something powerful might happen. Expect that something will happen and watch for it.

For Native Americans, entrances to the Sacred include ceremonies with sacred pipe, sweatlodge, vision quest, sun dance, but most importantly, just being in nature. What makes Red Path part of the spirit and tradition of Zen is that we place zazen as the foundation for our practice. Nothing takes the place of sitting zazen. Zazen is similar to Woman Prayer but goes a step beyond. It opens us to change and a new way of being in the world.

The purpose of zazen is to help us awaken to Oneness and how all things are interconnected. We are freed from fear and suffering by experiencing how this Oneness is our very own nature. Then, we need to refine bodymind and character so that we can live moment by moment in Oneness in the everyday world of differences. Over time we learn about ourselves, how we are constructing our own reality. Through practice we open to a wider range of perspectives, have more control over our actions, and live more consistently in a flow of love and harmony with all creation. This, however, takes more than flowery words.

Great Master Nansen was walking with a senior lay disciple, a high administrator in the Chinese government. His disciple quoted a famous poem "Heaven and earth and I are of the same root. All things and I are of the same substance," then added "Isn't that wonderful!"

Nansen pointed to a dandelion and said, "People of these days see this flower as though they were in a dream." Nansen's disciple was quoting a beautiful idea. Great Master Nansen through training and realization and more training was able to be that dandelion in its uniqueness and unity with all creation. When I hold my pipe and point west, I am the Pipe, the west, dandelion and sage.

Let's begin with the basics - how to settle body, breath, and mind. Meditation is a physical exercise as well as mental discipline. Proper alignment of the body and slow, deep breathing relaxes the muscles and helps open the joints and circulate healing energy throughout the system. The first rule of thumb is to sit comfortably with the belly free to breathe and the back straight, the legs and hands resting comfortably. There are a number of ways to do that.

In a Zen training hall, called a zendo, there is usually a collection of zafus and zabutons. A zafu is a small, round cushion that is placed on a rectangular, stuffed mat (zabuton). The cushion raises the body enough to be fairly comfortable to sit in a cross-legged position. The mat protects the ankles from resting on a hard floor. If one is capable, sitting in a full, half, or quarter lotus position is excellent. These forms provide the most stable platform for extended sitting. Most western-ers, particularly elderly ones like me, are not able to hike their feet up onto their thighs.

I well remember my first five day retreat in a Korean Zendo. I had not yet met Roshi Genki and the Zen Garland folk. I was totally naive. Having been used to my kind of meditation, I thought this would be a snap. The first half hour was wonderful. By the end of the second half hour, I was uncomfortable. During the third half hour my knees and low back were killing me. All my awareness was focused on pain.

For my part, sitting on the cushion is fine for a period or two of zazen. Longer than that, I go to a chair. I place a zafu on the chair in order to raise my buttocks higher than my knees, so that my stomach isn't cramped. This helps deepen my breathing and keeps my back straight. It is easier to meditate for longer periods if the spine is erect and the shoulders back so that the body is balanced.

There are internet sources for kneeling benches, which for some people are easier on the feet, knees, and thighs. Sitting on a chair is also an honorable and effective way to meditate.

It is recommended that you sit erect without being rigid so that your spine can offer an unobstructed flow of energy. Put your tongue on the roof of your mouth behind the upper teeth. Close your lips and teeth gently. Swallow one time to create a partial vacuum in your mouth. Breathe through your nose. Allow your eyelids to half close and focus your gaze on the floor four feet in front of you.

I love the sound of the gong and I ride that sound down into still-ness, so it is not "that" sound but the sound in me and is me. So, too, when I hold the sacred pipe, eventually I feel the heartbeat of the Grandmother in my hands.

In meditation you will find that your mind is your biggest aggrava-tion. The mind is made to think and that is what it does. The more you try to force your mind into stillness, the more thoughts will force their way in. You cannot grind your self into quietness. Let the thoughts come. Accept them as part of you, but try not to organize your time around them. If you notice them but don't dwell on them, they will drift away like clouds on a gentle breeze.

The Zen folks say, "put your mind in your belly." There is an energy point about an inch below the navel in the front of the low belly just above the pubis. When we put our attention there, feeling the breathing in the low belly, a special energy is generated. Hindus call it prana. Chinese call it ehi, and the Japanese call it Ki. This is a powerfully healing energy and in meditation can guide us to go deep within.

Allow yourself to dissolve into the breathing in the low belly, not observing it, but becoming breathing itself. Then gradually, over time and practice, body, mind, and self will fall away. This is a deep state Zen folks call Samadhi, or meditative oneness.

Now most of us will have difficulty keeping our attention in the low belly. People tell me "Oh, I can't meditate." But by regular practice, sitting quietly, focusing on our breathing, we train ourselves to persist even in difficulty. Practicing with breath in meditation builds the skills to be more present moment to moment in our daily lives. This amounts to being more alive. Some find it helpful to count their breaths. Others use a quiet mantra, a repetitive sentence such as "Om mani padme hum." Use whatever works for you to quiet your obsessive thinking.

Sit in meditation for five, ten, fifteen, twenty, or twenty-five minutes. When you are finished, you will know it. One of my students recently told me that she had planned to meditate for twenty minutes. She did not set a timer, and she came to an hour and twenty minutes later. It had been a blissful time for her.

In group zazen, we often use an Indian hand drum. Many people find that they go deeper in meditation with the drum. The drum is the heartbeat of Grandmother Earth. It helps us become one with Her and open to Her energy. Often at a pow- wow, an Indian baby will become fussy and start crying, but when the pow-wow drums start, the child quietens down. Why? Because that baby had been listening to the mother's heartbeat for nine months. Baby is home, hearing it again.

Pay attention to the sound of the drum. In-between the beats, you can hear the Om which is the sound of the earth. That sound comes from deep, deep within the Grandmother Earth, from way down in Her core. It is the sacred Om revered in Eastern religions. You can hear it in the drum.

You can also use the drum for your personal meditation although it can be problematic if you focus on the beating rather than on meditating. I have been doing it so long in ceremony that I scarcely think about it. If you are beating the drum for a group meditation, keeping a steady beat is essential. Irregular drumbeats pull the listener away from meditation and to the drum itself. In Red Path Zen sanghas drumming meditation is always followed by traditional zazen.

Red Path Zen also emphasizes walking meditation in the woods if possible. Once again, the focus is on meditation rather than the simple act of walking. Priscilla and I spend hours each week, hiking in the woods with our two Shelties. We do not walk together. We seldom talk. I want to be present to the woods, the trees, the animals. I feel the trees. I hear them. Their energy is smooth and healing. I absorb their energy and hopefully leave a trail of my positive energy behind.

Of course, there are times when I get lost in thought, when I am planning or reminiscing, or worrying. Upon returning to the present, I realize that I haven't perceived a thing along the path. There is a real difference between seeing and perceiving. You can see the path clearly, but have no memory of perceiving anything for whole periods of time.

Take time to stop walking. Pay attention! Listen! You may be delighted to find something happening between you and a tree, something totally outside your ordinary experience. Red Path Zen may change your life so that you can uncover your deep and essential spiritual nature which Zen calls your Buddha within.

CHAPTER 12

STALKING THE GREAT WHITE BULL BUFFALO

A Native retelling of the ancient "Searching for the Ox" story

The chill of early Fall permeated the night. Grandmother moon smiled down on a small village of tipis huddled in a close circle, the night's quietness punctuated only by the faint neighing of horses in a nearby corral and the singing night birds.

In one tipi, Lone Wolf and his bride, Turtle Woman, snuggled deep in their bed of buffalo and bear skin blankets. She lay tight against his body, secure in the warmth of his arms around her. But only she was asleep.

Lone Wolf's eyes were wide open in wonderment and worry.

He whispered: "Little one, are you awake?"

She answered: "You crazy? It's the middle of the night."

"For the past seven nights I have seen a big, white, bull buffalo in my dreams, and he keeps calling for me. "

She said, "Do you think they are power dreams?"

"I don't know for sure. It feels so."

Being a practical, but sleepy, young woman, she suggested, "Whatever it is, it can wait until morning. Tomorrow, go ask Bucking Horse, the medicine man, what he thinks."

Lone Wolf had been married long enough to know that the conversation was finished for the night. He pulled her tightly to himself and slipped into uneasy sleep.

The next morning just as soon as Bucking Horse's woman had built up their cooking fire, Lone Wolf, tobacco bag in hand, descended on the old Medicine Man. One always gives tobacco to the elder or medicine person from whom he is asking a favor.

Offering the tobacco to the old man, he said, "Grandfather, I have a question to ask."

"What is that, my son?"

"For the past seven nights I have dreamed of a big, white, bull buffalo. He keeps telling me to come to him. What does this mean? Is this a power dream?"

The old man said, "Tonight we will do a sweatlodge ceremony. Be there and ask your question of the Spirits. They may tell you what this white buffalo means."

Lone Wolf thought the day would never pass. He repaired everything that needed attention around the tipi. He worked over his quiver of arrows to make sure they were perfectly straight and feathered. He checked his horses to be sure they were fit. He was grumpy and unhelpful. Turtle Woman adored him even though she was aware that sometimes he could be a pain . . . like now when he was so inpatient.

Finally, it was time to prepare the sweatlodge ceremony. Lone Wolf was right there helping the fire tender select stones and lay the sacred fire. Lone Wolf had been given a sacred pipe a couple years earlier, so it was part of his spiritual work to learn how to build the sacred fire and make sure everything was ready for the ceremony. After an eternity spent waiting for the stones to become red hot, the men stripped down to their loin cloths and crawled into the sweatlodge.

When it was time, Bucking Horse said, "Ask the Spirits your question."

"Oh, Grandfathers of all the directions, hear me, your grandson, Lone Wolf. For the past seven nights I have dreamed of a white, bull buffalo who tells me to come to him. Is this something I should do? My heart tells me I should. I feel a big empty space inside my heart, and I long to have it filled. I have a wonderful wife and I love her very much, but I still have this yearning for something. I don't know what. Now, this white buffalo is calling me for some reason. Please help me."

Bucking Horse was silent as the men chanted a pipe song. When they were finished, he spoke, "Spirits say it is a Wakan (sacred) Buffalo calling you. You must find it. It will not be easy. Your determination must be firm and steady. If you succeed, you must tame it so that you can bring it back here to your people. If you succeed, you will bring great blessings to yourself, your family, and your tribe. Life has been hard for your people. They have forgotten how to laugh. They have forgotten how to be human beings. Maybe you will bring the people back to the Red Path."

"Aho! Wopila (thank you), Grandfathers. I will leave as soon as I can and search for this sacred beast who may bless our people."

Word spread quickly among the tipis that Lone Wolf would begin a search for a great white, buffalo wakan. Some warned that it was a fool's journey, that there was no such thing. What kind of idiot would put such effort into a dream buffalo?

Others brought him food and supplies to sustain him on his quest. They brought much more than he could use, for he would go on foot, not by horseback, packing just what he would need. The next day he started out at sunrise. The village gathered to see him off. His younger brother assured him that he would watch out for Turtle Woman, who stood stoically, choking back tears and praying silently that her man would return safely.

It soon became apparent to Lone Wolf that he had an impossible job. The prairie was full of buffalo. Buffalo family groupings were everywhere. One had to watch his step carefully for the ground had many piles of buffalo poop. Buffalo chips are an especially appreciated gift from the buffalo nation. When it is dried, it feeds the fires for cooking and warming the tipis. It was a regular task to gather dried chips and keep them covered and ready to burn.

So he walked carefully all day.

"How will I ever pick out a White Buffalo when there are so many herds? He could be hidden right in front of me and I would never see him."

Nevertheless, he continued wandering, walking, walking, walking in a generally westward direction, for the old ones teach that visions and sacred things come from the Grandfather of the West.

He was becoming very tired and discouraged. Maybe the doubters were right. This is a fool's journey. He stuck a piece of jerky in his mouth to satisfy his hunger, straightened his back, remembering Bucking Horse's admonishment to be determined. His feet were beyond being tired. He was a warrior, used to riding his pony everywhere. This continual walking was tearing up his legs and feet.

Toward dusk he began planning where to stop for the night, when something caught his eye.

"Whoa! What is that? Ah, it is buffalo dung, but there is a strange shimmering to it."

Bent over for a clearer view, he saw it was indeed poop. It didn't seem like the other dung around it. It glowed.

"This is crazy!" he thought. "What has that buffalo been eating?"

And then he thought, "Maybe it is a sign. I will follow this poop trail and see where it leads."

Way into the night he followed the shimmering scat until he could go no farther. Curling up in his blanket, he drifted off to sleep in the chilly night beneath a starlit sky.

The first light awakened him. Grabbing a piece of jerky for a breakfast, he started off again, following the trail of shimmering poop. It seemed there would be no end to it. And then, way ahead, he thought he saw movement.

He had seen this place before. It was a small river with cottonwood trees along its bank. A mist had risen from the river and he couldn't see clearly, but he thought he saw movement. He couldn't be sure.

But wait! He saw it again. Then it emerged from the fog.

"That's it. That's my buffalo, a huge white buffalo. That's my buffalo." He was nearly shouting in excitement. "Aho!"

But just as quickly, the buffalo disappeared into the mist and was gone. The young man ran to the creek, eagerly looking first to his right and then to his left.

"I know I saw him right here. He's not going to get away from me. I'm going to get you, big fella."

Once again, the mist lifted just enough for Lone Wolf to see the buffalo. The question was, how to capture the sacred beast? Everyone knows you can't just lasso a buffalo if you favor your life. He knew he had to bring the White Buffalo back to the village. Those instructions were very clear.

"Maybe I can, though," he thought. "He called me to come to him in my dreams. If I am going to bring him back with me, what other choice do I have? I will give it a try."

Now he was scared. He had hunted buffalo ever since he was old enough to pull a bow. He knew how dangerous these animals could be. But he had to take the chance.

Unwinding his lasso and swinging it in a gentle arc, he prepared to settle the loop over the buffalo's neck. Just then the buffalo jerked up his massive head, glaring at Lone Wolf. Snorting fire from his great nostrils, his eyes blazed red.

"Holy shit!" screamed Lone Wolf. He began to run backwards to a cottonwood tree. Grabbing a branch, he scrambled as high as he could.

"Now what am I supposed to do?"

The great white buffalo strolled over and bumped the tree a couple of times, just enough to terrify Lone Wolf. Perhaps he was warning the little human that he better be more respectful than to think he could capture this buffalo with a rope.

It seemed hours before the buffalo backed off a bit, and Lone Wolf could descend from his tree. Now what to do? The buffalo appeared to have no intention of leaving the area. He stood at a distance keeping a wary eye on the human.

It suddenly dawned on Lone Wolf that if he couldn't capture the buffalo, he would have to win its trust. He must take a very different tack. The buffalo was obviously wakan, so Lone Wolf decided to approach it in a sacred way.

Kneeling on the ground, he cleared a space for his sacred bundle which held his chanupa wakan (sacred prayer pipe). Opening the bundle, he put his pipe together and pointed the stem at the buffalo. He prayed, "Oh Grandfather Buffalo, you called me in my dreams and I have come. Please tell me what I must do so that you will come with me to my village.

Filling the pipe with knicknick (tobacco), he began to chant all the sacred songs he had learned. After what seemed to be hours, the buffalo came and stood next to him, bobbing his head in rhythm to the songs. As Lone Wolf sang, the atmosphere settled and the earth became quiet. A strange calmness permeated the whole area.

Finally, Lone Wolf lit the sacred pipe, offered it to the Grandfathers of all the directions, and to the great white buffalo wakan. The young man felt a change happening inside him. Everything was different somehow. The cottonwood tree next to him seemed to open its arms toward him, welcoming him. Even the raucous crows were screeching in a lovely way, "Welcome little brother."

Lone Wolf carefully took his pipe apart, blew out the ashes, and folded it back into his bundle. He stood up and dared lean carefully against the buffalo's side feeling the tremendous power in this great animal. How different this was than before when the buffalo had chased him up the tree. Now there was a gentleness, a kind of mutual appreciation. Lone Wolf didn't know what to make of this, but did not destroy the moment by questioning it. He knew the Sacred One in a way beyond understanding.

They began to walk side by side back towards the village. Lone Wolf was very tired, worn out by the energy spent hunting the beast, hiding in the tree, and now beginning the long journey home.

After a while the buffalo spoke, "Little human, you are very tired. Why don't you climb up on my back and I will carry you, for I know where to find your village."

Lone Wolf was awed at this invitation, and maybe a little scared but too fatigued to hesitate. So, grabbing two fists full of buffalo mane, he jumped astride. To his relief the buffalo let him settle down before he gently loped toward the village.

As they neared the circle of tipis, Lone Wolf began to sing out the song with which one warns the village that he is approaching, and that he means no harm. This was the custom among the people. They didn't like to be surprised by uninvited visitors. Lone Wolf needed to identify himself.

There was a general rustle as villagers emerged from their tipis and the horse coral.

But what was this? Beyond belief and to his astonishment, all the villagers were small white buffalos. His mind blown, he could barely hold his seat astride the great White. The village "buffalos" began to press around him and the Sacred White, and as Lone Wolf gazed down on them, he saw that his legs were covered with white fur, and his feet were hooves. Strangely, it somehow felt very natural to him.

He realized he was looking down through the eyes of the great white. No! He himself was the Great White Bull Buffalo. All the village buffalos were merging with him. They were all the Great White Sacred Buffalo.

Then, they were no longer buffalo . . . They were no longer . . . they were just clear white . . . no Lone Wolf, no buffalo, no village.

Who knows how long this continued. Hours? How would Lone Wolf know? He did not exist. He was beyond knowing, beyond presence, beyond self. One.

In the distance a voice penetrated the emptiness. Bucking Horse was singing a welcoming song calling the people together. Forms began to emerge. Forms took shape as recognizable human beings. There was Turtle Woman with a huge smile on her face, and there was Bucking Horse, and his little brother, all his extended family, wreathed in welcoming smiles. Lone Wolf recognized himself. The great White Buffalo was gone.

The people pressed around him, eager for details of his journey. All they knew was that Lone Wolf had come walking back into their midst while singing his "It's me coming home" song.

"Tell us what happened. Did you see a White Buffalo?"

"Not now," he said. "I have to talk with Bucking Horse first, and he will probably want to do a sweatlodge and consult the Spirits. This has been a very weird time."

So the people slapped him on the back and told him how happy they were that he had come home safely. Somehow, they knew that he had changed. Somehow, they felt a change in themselves. They wondered about Lone Wolf. You could tell he was a little different.

But it was still the young warrior, Lone Wolf, who took Turtle Woman by the hand, led her into the tipi, and fastened the flap behind them. They fell into their blankets, and the space was filled with giggles and sounds of great pleasure.

Much later, grinning, maybe a bit self-consciously, he emerged from the tipi and joined the other young men in building a huge fire. The drums began to call the people who soon appeared wearing their fancy outfits. This night would be full of dancing and thanksgiving.

It had been a very long time since the village had danced and felt such a deep sense of community. They could not account for it, but in the Indian way, "accounting" was not important. Enjoyment was. Like our old friend, Sky Dreamer, they partied when they could and they partied when they couldn't.

And so it was.

Aho! Mitakuye Oyas'in

CHAPTER 13

LISTENING

The importance of listening was brought home to me many years ago during my four day/four night vision quest when my Spirit teacher came to me. It was the second night. Until then it had been a quiet vision quest with nothing much happening. Chanupa wakan firmly in my hands, I prayed, "Ho, Grandfather, please, before this quest is over I want to learn about my stone man."

I must digress here to describe what I mean by the term "stone man." Some years earlier I had been diagnosed with stomach ulcers. I followed the treatment prescribed by a physician. Later, I returned to the physician and found that the stomach ulcers were gone but I had a mysterious mass in my intestine below the stomach. The doctor immediately wanted to do a biopsy to ascertain the nature of this lump.

I told the doctor that I wanted to check with my consultant first. When he pressed me to find out what I meant by that, I confessed that my consultant was my medicine man, George White Wolf. My physician sarcastically told me that these lumps did not just disappear, that no witch doctor could get rid of it, and that if a witch doctor cured this he would send him all of his patients.

"Nevertheless," I said, "This is what I want to do." As soon as I got home, I called White Wolf and told him what had happened. He instructed me to come immediately to his place where he would put up a sweatlodge ceremony, and ask the Spirits what needed to be done. The fire was already burning brightly and the stones almost ready by the time I arrived. Before long, Whitewolf and I were in the lodge, listening to the water sizzle into steam and singing the familiar sweatlodge songs.

At the appropriate time, Whitewolf explained to the Spirits what had happened and asked what I needed to do. The Spirits instructed me to perform a pipe ceremony three times a day and to drink a certain tea for one week. At the end of the week I was to have another set of x-rays. If the tumor was gone, that would be good. If not, I would need to do the white man's medicine. This was a very typical prescription from the Spirits. There is nothing wrong with White man's medicine if you need it.

The Youth Services Bureau (a mental health agency for children, youth and their families) where I was executive director sat on a wooded piece of land, so it was easy to get away and pray three times a day and drink the prescribed tea. As I cradled the chanupa and prayed, I also held in my hand a certain red crystalline stone which came from an earlier sweatlodge. The stone began to shiver in my hand almost like Jell-O. There was something strange and powerful in that stone.

When I told my doctor that I would want to do more x-rays at the end of the week, he objected saying that would be too much for my body. When I insisted, he relented and ordered the x-rays. Returning to the radiologist's office, I once again drank the barium, and had the x-rays. The mass had disappeared.

That evening the physician called and said that something was wrong with the x-rays and he wanted me to go to the hospital the next morning to have yet another set of x-rays, this time under special conditions. When I demurred, reminding him that he had cautioned about too much x-ray exposure, he assured me that it wouldn't be a problem. It would be "like a day in the sunshine." So, I had a new set of x-rays. No mass.

As you might guess, the physician never sent any patients to Whitewolf.

In the following sweatlodge, the Spirits, through White Wolf, told me that the quivering stone was my stone man and gave me his name, *Ishnala Mani*. The red stone would be my connection with him until the time came for me to know him directly. For several years after that I knew nothing more about Ishnala Mani other than what had been told me in the ceremony.

Years later, Whitewolf put me on the hill for my fourth vision quest. A four day/four night vision quest is very difficult as it is done without food, water, or shelter. By the second night when nothing much had happened, I asked, "Ho, Grandfather, I have been wearing this stone man around my neck for years. Before this vision quest is finished, I would like to learn more about him."

A strong voice behind me said, "What do you want to know?"

Startled, I almost jumped out of my skin and nearly threw my chanupa over my head. Not knowing what else to say, I stammered, "Well, Grandfather, I would like to see you."

Immediately this ancient, Indian face with a wicked smile loomed right in front of me and said, "How's that?"

"Grandfather, I would like to see all of you."

Immediately, an Indian man manifested himself in front of me wearing jeans and a plaid shirt, turning in a slow dance so that I could see all of him. With a big grin he asked, "How's that?"

"Thank you, Grandfather. "Please sit and smoke with me."

He sat down beside me and for several hours we talked. I was visiting with him in person just like I might sit with George Whitewolf. Understand that he was a Spirit, but He was visible to me. Our conversations were as natural as if he were just another human being. Grandfather Ishnala Mani returned the next two nights, teaching me songs and healing rituals, instructing me more about walking the Red Road, and giving me information about himself. I asked why he had chosen to work with me.

He laughed, "Because you were already a fool."

He had been a Heyoka (clown/trickster) medicine man way back before the White invasion, and I had been a clown most of my life. We were apparently well suited to each other.

On the last night of my vision quest, I was taken to a cave. Take my word for it. I was there in the cave, but was my body still sitting in the vision quest altar? Could it be that we have an alternate "body" which can travel separately from our physical body? It's an interesting question.

The cave's entrance was partially blocked by a rock slide. Inside, beyond the rocks, I could see an ugly kind of shimmering green light. It seemed to me that I should go no further because the path was blocked. Suddenly, Grandfather stepped from behind me. Taking my hand, he said "Come on" and helped me scramble over the boulders.

A hard-packed path led us farther into the cave. To the left of the path there were numerous pits. Upon closer examination the pits looked like opening mouths. Pointing at them, my teacher said that those were the sucking mouths of the people. He said, "Beware the demands of the people and the seduction of your ego. If you think you can be everything to the people, do everything for them, they will suck away your energy, pull you off the path and destroy you."

To the right side of the path, up beyond the rock slide, the nasty green light was beckoning.

My teacher spoke, "That light is the seductive power of evil. It will promise you everything and take away everything. Never ever use the power of evil even for what you consider to be positive purposes, for it will kill you."

Ahead, the path broadened into a much larger circular room in the center of which sat six older Indian men. Grandfather told me to wait just outside the room, and he entered to speak to these elders. I could tell that they were talking about me because they kept looking in my direction while speaking earnestly among themselves. Finally,

Grandfather returned and said that these six elders were my Spirit Teachers. They could not talk with me yet because I did not know how to listen. Grandfather stated that he would stay with me, teach me, and be their spokesman in working with me.

It took many years before these six Grandfathers would contact me directly, many years to learn how to listen. I had to slow down, still my racing mind, and pay attention. Until then, there was no chance that I could really hear or understand them.

Modern people live at a frantic pace. The problem of never being quiet in the mind was not mine alone; it is a malady for most all of us. An old Zen master called it, "the Monkey mind." We get up in the morning to the sound of TV. We race through the day in endless activity. We watch the evening news and other shows, turn off the lights and go to sleep without ever spending a moment quietly paying attention, listening. No wonder we seldom hear the voices of our ancestors. No wonder the Spirits cannot speak to us. How could They get a word in edgewise?

As a young man I used to wonder about my father. He had spent his life as a Protestant minister until he retired to a small home on a lake in Florida. He still lived a very active lifestyle, but he would spend an hour or two every afternoon quietly looking out over the lake, watching the seabirds and the resident alligator, just being still. At the time it seemed to me like such a waste. Now I know that it was probably his most productive period of the day.

If you want to connect more deeply with the Sacred, I would recommend that you commit to zazen every day and *expect* your spiritual life to change and deepen.

Incidentally, I am not the only one who has Spirit teachers. You have them as well. The regular practice of silence makes room for you and your Spirit Teachers to become One.

CHAPTER **14**

DANCING THE NEW DAY

Imagine yourself sitting in an Indian sweatlodge (inipi) ceremony. It is blacker than a thousand midnights in the piney woods. You are knee to knee with ten other participants, listening to water sizzle on red hot stones. The temperature has climbed to 160 degrees. The Spirits have announced their presence with tiny sparkling lights like miniature lightning bugs.

One of your fellows is praying. "Ho, Tunkashila (Grandfather) have pity on me. I want very much to be spiritual, to be able to walk each day in balance and in beauty. Please help me."

The Spirits once answered such a prayer, "Greet each morning with dance. Be grateful for the new day, a new chance to live and be a human being." We couldn't help but laugh at the idea of greeting the day with a dance. I am too old and stiff for such things, and my woman may not be so old, but her joints don't work that well first thing in the morning.

Of course, that wasn't what the Spirits meant. The dance is to greet each new day with joy and excitement. The day is full of promise. If you want to walk spiritually, then you must take those first steps. Greet the day with gratitude.

Each morning I face the new sun, standing in presence with the trees, winged ones, and four-leggeds around me and make my prayers for the day. There is a special place outside, surrounded by woods and wildlife where I go to greet the day. Statues of the Buddha occupy special places in our woods and I greet them with respect.

My prayer goes something like this: "Hau, Grandfather. Thank you for this new day. Help me to live it in a good way, to live it like a human being. Help me walk in balance. Let me walk with Beauty in front of me, Beauty behind me, Beauty above me and Beauty beneath my feet. Help me live in love, gratitude, and with a deepening sense of Oneness. Let me be a hollow bone through which your healing and love can flow to the world around me and through which I can receive healing and love from the Creation."

To walk in balance means to be centered with yourself and all your relations (human beings, trees, animals, waters etc.), to experience light, quietness, joy in your heart. The opposite of balance is to be irritated, angry, resentful, fearful, and depressed. These are all emotions that create barriers and close you off from others.

Whenever you are out of balance, go outside and look around you. Remind yourself that you are just one of the many beings that belong here, and that *you* also belong here. Breathe deeply a few times. Speak to the Spirits and say "Thank you for my life." Smile even if you don't feel like it at first, because doing these things will lift your mood and open your eyes to beauty and healing and love.

The morning dance prepares you, over time, to become a hollow bone through which the positive, healing energy of Grandmother Earth can flow through you and out to all your relations. And, it allows you to reabsorb the love and energy from all the brother and sister nations around you, the plants, the animals. Be aware, though, that to be a hollow bone means that you must be free, open, and loving as possible, freed from negativity. An effective hollow bone is an open bone.

There are several quiet places in our house graced by small altars and sitting Buddhas. There is one where I usually sit for private zazen. Others are more of a reminder to me to stay mindful. There is also the Sangha room with its more elaborate altar including the Buddha, a buffalo skull, and deer hide. The altar is completed with a fresh flower, water, candle and incense. These sacred spots are continual reminders that I am a hollow bone for all creation around me.

One sunny afternoon I was driving along the interstate, when a morning prayer chant entered my mind. I have no sense that it was a private song for me alone, or that you have to be Indian or a sojourner on the Red Road to use it. It works well with a drum and just as well without one. Try facing the morning sun and sing this chant. You can create your own simple melody. Your heart will give it to you.

Thank you for this day.
> Thank you for this day.
Thank you for another day
> to live and to share

Thank you for this day.
> Thank you for this day.
Thank you for another day
> To love and to care.

Let me walk in balance.
> Let me walk in balance.
Let me walk in balance
> For another day.
>> (Repeat twice)

Beauty before me.
> Beauty behind me.
Beauty above me,
> and Beauty beneath my feet.
>> (Repeat twice)

Thank you for this day.
> Thank you for this day.
Thank you for another day
> To live and to share.

Thank you for this day.
> Thank you for this day.
Thank you for another day
> To love and to care.

Dance each new day. Practice gratitude and walking in beauty. Your spirituality will deepen exponentially.

CHAPTER 15

SPIRITS

Someone asked, "Do you believe in Spirits? If so, what are the differences or the similarities between the Spirits and God?

It is an important question. Who is more powerful, the Creator or the Spirits? Obviously, if there is a Creator, then It created everything, including the Spirits. But that is not the most relevant question. I think the more pertinent question is: With whom do we consult and work? The Creator, Spirits, or both?

I think we first must look at our definition of Creator. Do we see the Creator as the Old Man in the Heavens, the Grandfather of all Grandfathers? Before the missionaries came, the Native people apparently did not think much at all about the nature of God. They had no words to describe whatever that supreme Deity might be. They didn't think of a male or female God of all Gods. They contented themselves to use the term, Wakan Tanka, the Great Mystery. They preferred to work with the Spirits whom they could hear and with whom they could interact, and from whom they could get help.

I, myself, do not believe in a personified God. More technically, I would be called a pantheist. I don't think that God is made in the image of Man. I don't believe that whatever God may be is involved in our lives and is managing our destiny. I don't believe that God chooses one person to be Hitler and another to be Ghandi. But I deeply believe that all Creation, known and unknown, is sacred, and that by extension we are all sacred, all are God.

I think that the best term for God is, Wakan Tanka, and that when the Great Mystery expressed Itself, It created the world in Its own image, and I think that image is Mitakuye Oyas'in, which we Buddhists call Oneness. The Great Mystery provided the spark to creation which manifests in great diversity. Always a tension exists between the pull to essential Oneness and the illusion of our separateness.

The whole creation is striving in its own evolutionary way to realize the Oneness which is its essence. This is the task of the Spirit world and our world. Each Spirit has its own agenda to realize Oneness. We have our own life purpose to bring Oneness to the world, to participate in the ongoing creation, so that everything we do is in the name of Mitakuye Oyas'in. None of us ever does this perfectly, but some do more than others. Many people have no idea that this is a purpose in their lives, but to me, this is the Bodhisattva path.

So, realizing Oneness in my own life and sphere of influence has become my over arching purpose. To that end, I listen to the Spirits. My teacher, Ishnala Mani, has been a constant guide and source of inspiration. Some times he or my other teachers will want me to do something which I would rather not do, but I generally acquiesce because we are all serving Oneness, and They have a better perspective than I do, greater access to information than I have.

Are the Spirits infallible? Of course not. No Spirit guide that I know of has ever claimed to be infallible. We are all in this process together . . . to realize Oneness, Mitakuye Oyas'in. So, I listen to my Spirit teachers and generally cooperate with them. I try to live in a way that creates oneness with my fellow beings, human, animal, vegetable and mineral. I try to let go of those things that separate me.

Among those things are a judgmental attitude. When I find myself judging another person, it is generally because they are showing me things in myself that I abhor. Check this out. Think of the person in your world that you most dislike. What is it about him/her that turns you off? Now, look at yourself. Do you see any of those same traits in you?

I try to let go of judging because judging keeps me separate and is contrary to Mitakuye Oyas'in. It has been repeated by many writers that we judge others by their actions and ourselves by our best intentions. I find that to be very true.

In each situation requiring me to set a course of action, I try to choose the loving course. In these ways, I join the rest and best of Creation in bringing Mitakuye Oyas'in into human consciousness.

There are times when you say "no" to the Spirits. If what They are asking is more than you can do physically or emotionally, you have a right to say "no." Remember, They have work to do and see you as a co-worker, and They may not be as sensitive to your needs as you would like. You may decide that They aren't understanding your situation. If so, go by what you know is right, but you should look carefully at your reasons for disagreeing because your Spirit teachers generally know more than you do. I think it is most often when I am in a judgmental, angry stance that I want to say, "no."

The Spirits pulled me from the sweatlodge. That really hurt. I know that I am perfectly capable of sweating, but in the name of Oneness, they wanted me teaching in non-native settings. I was angry and hurt about this, but agreed to go along with it. Today I see clearly that I was and am now and will always carry the sweatlodge within me. I am One with the lodge even if I am not in the lodge. The Spirits also gave me the Sangha and the Dharma which elaborate and clarify all that I had learned in the Native way.

So, who is more powerful, God or the Spirits? In the Christian metaphor as told in the first chapter of the Gospel of John, we read, "In the beginning was the Word . . . and the Word was with God, and the Word was God . . . Through Him all things were made; without Him nothing was made that has been made."

I like the Native/Buddhist metaphors better. In the beginning was the Great Mystery that expressed Itself in Oneness (Mitakuye Oyas'in), and the Creation blossomed forth as an expression of that Oneness. Many of us, Red Men, Buddhists, and Christians, work with the Spirits, some of whom have had earlier existences as human beings in this dimension. We are all expressions of Wakan Tanka.

There are also ghost Spirits. These are people who were not able to make it over into the next dimension. They are stuck in this one usually because they were so attached to a place or certain people that they could not leave. Some are happy and content to be around us. Others may be holding strong negative emotions, and such ghosts can cause trouble.

Once, Priscilla and I were sleeping in a motel. I was awakened by racket coming from the bathroom. It sounded like paper being ripped and shredded. Jumping from bed, I hustled into the bathroom where I encountered a recently deceased woman in a furious state. I tried to reason with her, telling her that there would be guides to help her across to the next dimension, that she should look for a light to guide her. Nothing I said made an impact. Suddenly, my Spirit teacher, Ishnala Mani, tapped me on my shoulder saying, "You are over your head. Go back to bed. We will take care of this."

I was only too happy to comply. Returning to bed, I slept soundly. The next morning the angry ghost was gone.

A final word. As Red Path Zen Buddhists, we do not use Zazen or meditation as a portal to the Spirits. We certainly recognize and honor work with Spirits, Spirit Teachers, Guides and Medicine Helpers, and there are ceremonies that provide these opportunities such as the sweatlodge and sacred pipe ceremonies. Zazen and drumming meditation have a different purpose for us. It is a quiet time of receptiveness and, perhaps, the experience of Oneness. Spirits certainly may come while you are in meditation, and that is okay. The difference is that we don't use zazen as an opening to contact Spirits or do shamanic journeying. There are times when we have heard the

Spirits/Ancestors chanting with us in Sangha. It is such a gift when that happens, but again, hearing our Grandfathers join in our chants is not the goal of Zen meditation.

Shamanic journeying is irrelevant to enlightenment. It is a useful tool. It has existed in Zen and Native groups over the centuries. It is an honorable gift and has a place and purpose. I am often called upon to consult the Spirits by moving into another reality, but not while sitting zazen.

CHAPTER 16

SPIRIT COMMUNICATION

In the Indian world, we are comfortable discussing Spirit Communication. You hear the term, "Spirit told me to do this or that." It sounds awfully easy, rather trite, and often misleading. The question remains, "What does it mean to talk with Spirits?" Keep in mind that there are Good Spirits, Trickster Spirits, and yes, there are Evil Spirits.

When the leader of your community says that the Spirits told him to take a certain action, you have a right to know just what that means and how he could be so sure. We know that people have done awful things because "the Spirits told them so." Remember Jonestown.

Jim Jones began his ministry as a dedicated worker for civil rights and social justice. He had plenty of charisma and personal power. Little by little, he was seduced by his ego into claiming more and more power. He was listening to his Spirits, or was he? He began to think of himself as someone really special in his relationship with the Spirits. The community that gathered around him also bought into his personal myth and suffered horrible consequences. To work with shamanic powers or, in the native way of thinking, to work with the Spirits is a great blessing, a formidable responsibility, and a constant struggle with ego which always craves more. So, it is right to question. If you aren't sure, ask.

I can only describe how conversations with the Spirits happen for me. I cannot speak for anyone else. I am able to go into that "other world" when I need to know something or find out something for one of my community. That is my gift and responsibility as a medicine person.

There are three levels of confidence that I use for "testing the Spirits." Maybe I should say that there are three levels of confidence I use for testing my ego and being sure that what I am hearing is truly from the Spirits and not from my unconscious (or conscious) desires.

These are the three levels of communication, each having an increasing level of certainty:

Level 1

I think this is common to all of us. We get a strong impression that we should take a certain action. It is almost as if there is a hand on the shoulder urging us to listen. This is the level that is most common and most likely to be misunderstood. We get strong impressions about a lot of things. Most of the time the Grandfather Spirits are not involved. At this level it is necessary to be careful before taking action. Check it out. Ask yourself if it is right, ethical, or helpful to move ahead? Am I just hearing what I want to hear? Is this just an affirmation, an agreement with my preconceived notion? Is there anything new I wouldn't think of on my own? It is easy to be fooled at this level. The Christian Bible says that you must "test the Spirits." This is true.

At this level, many people see "signs" all around them. They will come to me in a lather of excitement saying, "I was driving my car and a hawk flew across the road in front of me. Is that a sign? Does that mean I have hawk medicine?" It usually means that the hawk is hungry, looking for a meal.   On the other hand, it just might be a sign. At this level don't take anything for granted. Your Red Path leader can help you with these things.

Level 2

Sometimes the Spirits speak with such a strong voice that we are stopped in our tracks. It sounds like the voice is outside us. We hear it with our ears, but there are no visual clues. If this happens for you, you will be struck by the alien feeling of the voice and its message. It feels non-self.

I mentioned earlier the time Priscilla and I were hiking with our Shelties and my teacher, Ishnala Mani, said, "Sweat Otterheart before you leave." That voice was loud and clear. I argued with it and was overruled. I checked it out in the sweatlodge and was told why I had gotten that command.

Several years ago I was awaked from a deep sleep and heard very strongly and clearly, "That was your last sweatlodge" referring to a ceremony the night before. I had no reason to expect that message and found it very disturbing.

So, I went to a deeper level the next day with my sacred pipe where I got the full story.

Level 3

It is a wonderful gift to have the experience of sitting in person with your Spirit teacher. On my fourth vision quest, my teacher joined me and sat beside me in the altar. We talked person to person. He gave me some excellent teaching and also gave me some sacred songs.

I have bet my life on the reality of this experience. For more than thirty years, I have followed his guidance. He is always beside me. He is always there when I have a question. I do not always see him, but I feel his presence and it is very comforting to me.

So, for me, when I get a communication that is level one, I always check it out. If it is level two, I check it out more quickly and pay a lot more attention. If it is level three, I am willing to bet my life on it.

CHAPTER 17

PRACTICAL SIDE OF SPIRITUALITY

Being a Hollow Bone

There have been times when I have wished to be a monk. I imagined sitting on my cushion, walking in the woods, living in holiness and meditation, and eating simple food. Life would be good; no worries, time to pray and meditate. What a pipe dream! Living the life of a monk involves a lot of hard work and sacrifice.

There is much more to Zen than the meditation cushion. Zazen is very important, but the full Zen inspired life is much more. I realize that sitting in zazen and achieving samadhi is the accepted, ultimate goal of Zen, but I think that a life of Oneness, of loving service, of giving oneself for the good of all Creation is the ultimate gift. That to me is the goal of the Bodhisattva vows. Of course, sitting zazen creates the internal attitudes and openness to live the Bodhisattva way.

As mentioned earlier, I greet each morning with prayer, and my prayers end with my asking the Spirits to help me be a hollow bone. To be a hollow bone is to be an open, healing and loving person. As we walk down the street or in a shopping center or deep in the woods, we leave a trail of positive energy behind us . . . or negative energy. You have met people who make you feel good by just having contact with them. You also have been around others who cause your defenses to rise. Perhaps they were hostile or just negative. I think most people fall into yet another category. They are pretty much ciphers. They don't affect you one way or another.

When you are "on" as a hollow bone, you are channeling positive energy without even thinking about it.

A hollow bone has an added dimension. The love and healing energy flows both directions: out to the world and back to you. When we are open, we can draw a great deal of healing energy, love and effective power back into ourselves. It is a two way street.

To be an open conduit, a bone must be hollow. It can't be filled with suspicion, hatred, jealousy, judgement, or the abuse of power. Sitting in Zazen doesn't necessarily free you from negative emotions. It is unfortunately true that spiritual people can be abusive and ethically challenged. They may be high and holy at times but are not necessarily hollow bones. The seduction of the ego is an ever present danger, especially to those seen as spiritual leaders.

Being Clear

For this reason we urge our people to deal with the issues that in many cases they have tried to avoid. Most everyone has life problems that have plagued them since childhood. Many of us have faced these problems in therapy, and they no longer get in the way of our spiritual lives. But, this is not always true.

For those who have been through therapy and have dealt with their problems, we congratulate them. For others we recommend that they experience the process called Focusing which is not a professional therapy but a way that regular folk can contact and resolve their internal conflicts. I have seen powerful results as Zen folk have used focusing to de-fang their past traumas and hangups.

We have seen too many priests, too many Roshis, too many Rimpoches who have been pulled off the spiritual track because of unresolved needs and problems. Of course, this is not only true of Buddhist leaders, but also of Christian and other clergy. Abuses should not happen and will not happen if we honestly look at ourselves, and seriously prepare to be truly hollow bones for the people.

Some Buddhist groups are beginning to bring Western psychological processes into their practice. Zen Garland is committed to making such a process (focusing) available as a core practice for the sangha.

Practicing Community

From its beginnings, Zen was most often practiced in a monastic community. To be Zen was tantamount to being a monk or nun. In the US and Europe, Zen is evolving more and more into a lay movement. This requires us to rethink the notion of community. In both traditional Zen and Native American worlds, community was at the heart of spirituality and spirituality was experienced within community.

Perhaps the best metaphor for community is the good family. It is a place where we feel at home and valued; where there are people we can trust to guard our backs. When we are needy, the community is there for us and vice versa.

There was a time in our mother zendo when a member was critically ill and in the hospital for a period of time. She did not have personal family to care for her. Our Roshi and other community members took turns sitting with her in the hospital night and day. When she was released, the Zen community fed and cared for her. This is an expression of love and Oneness. This is real community.

We are moving into a time when our world may face financial collapse and there may be a struggle for food and shelter. If this should happen, community will be essential for survival. When I started the first Red Path Zen Sangha, I wanted it to be made of neighbors. I felt that in the coming times, if neighbors had a sense of community, we could care for each other.

Modern Zen practitioners in the West have embraced something called Socially Engaged Buddhism that has emphasized the need to get off the cushion regularly and care for the most needy and marginalized. Zen groups are operating food pantries and providing regular meals for the homeless.

As a service, the Zen Garland Order has adopted Charity Oasis: A Haven for Women and Children in Paterson, New Jersey. Roshi Ann Ankai Wagner was a founder of this program that educates poor women and provides meals, clothing and food for them and their children.

We also minister to jailed migrants who have no right to legal representation and are treated with shameless disregard. They are held for long periods of time with no resolution or pathway toward release or even deportation. Our people meet with them and do what we can to humanize their situation.

One of our Zen Garland priests, Dr. Joanne Cacciatore, is the founder of the MISS Foundation. She is a nationally recognized expert in the field of traumatic death and her foundation is educating and supporting people around the world in ways of dealing with traumatic death.

There is no end to need. Out of our sense of Oneness we do what we can. We are manifesting community.

Unfortunately, community cannot be legislated. It is not born of fiat. It must develop organically. As we sit together regularly and pray together, a closeness and understanding begins to develop. This can be nourished by meals together, hiking together, and sharing life outside the Zendo. It takes time and effort, but will be worth it. For followers of Red Path Zen, the sacred pipe and inipi ceremonies enhance community building.

Physical Discipline

Zen has always recognized the importance of bringing the body and mind together. So long as we are in this life, the two are one. Understanding that Mind and Body are one, Zen urges the practice of physical discipline. From the most ancient times yoga has been a chosen form, for it encourages focus, mindfulness, and physical discipline. Today, Akido holds an important place in Zen Garland, but there are other arts such as Tai Chi and Qi Gong which are also available.

The key in all these practices is to create balance between body and mind to bring you into presence with what you are doing. It is like meditation in motion. In our retreats, long periods of meditation are broken up with movement, most often yoga, but sometimes just simple stretching. After sitting a couple of hours with brief periods of walking meditation, it is a gift to have an hour of yoga and stretching. It is good for body and soul.

For earlier generations native spiritual practices did not include things like yoga to bring you to mindfulness because mindfulness was necessary for survival. Imagine how important it was to be one with your horse and focused on the hunt, especially if the prey were buffalo. This was dangerous hunting. Survival depended on total focus, and any loss of focus could mean death for both you and your pony. This was true in so much early tribal life when danger was always present. There was no time to waste in fantasy. This is no longer the case, and native people entering the Sangha have the same problems as Anglos. In this way, traditional Zen enriches Red Path Zen.

PART 3

NATIVE TRADITIONAL CEREMONIES

CHAPTER 18

CAVEAT

As I open this section on native traditional ceremonies: sacred pipe (chanupa wakan), sweatlodge (inipi), and vision quest (hanblecheya), I feel a need to take off my shoes. These ceremonies are the most sacred, the most holy, the most honored ceremonies of the people, and they must be approached with deepest reverence.

These ceremonies are also most problematic for Red Path Zen because they are not widely available to our people. This very fact is part of the reason that the Grandfathers sent me to teach outside native communities. People need a way to approach the Sacred, a way that is universally accessible. Traditional Zen Sanghas are there for everyone. The big three Native ceremonies are not.

In all honesty we have to be very careful and respectful about incorporating the pipe, inipi, and vision quest into a spiritual community not organically connected to the Lakota people who are understandably wary of outsiders appropriating their sacred rites. You will hear, "The White Man has stolen our land and nearly destroyed our people. Now they are stealing our religion." It is incumbent on us to require that leaders who use these rites have the training and experience to use them correctly and to observe the ways of respect in approaching them. Red Path Zen must be rooted in a native lineage just as it is rooted in the linage of Shakyamuni.

While our Native ceremonies are not yet widely accessible, a few people are training to become pipe carriers. Undoubtably, inipi and vision quest leaders will come in the future. Leadership must grow in the slow steady process typical in traditional native communities. One does not become trained or authorized to lead any of the ceremonies by reading a book or attending a few ceremonies. For instance persons trying to pour water (inipi) without appropriate understanding of the ceremony or the training necessary to do it safely can actually hurt people. Remember the awful situation in Arizona where a New Age guru, without the necessary skills and understanding, accidentally killed several people in a sweatlodge and sickened even more. His sweatlodge bore little or no resemblance to an inipi ceremony.

Modern folk tend to think in terms of specific steps which one takes to achieve a goal, and that these steps can be shortened. They would want Sacred Pipe 101 and three months later Sacred Pipe 102. A young man once appeared in Whitewolf's camp, and after a couple of sweats stated that he wanted to become a medicine man.

Whitewolf answered, "That's good," but said nothing more. A bit later the young man insisted that he needed to know how fast he could become a medicine person.

Exasperated, Whitewolf said, "You will have to do a thousand sweats before you are there."

A month or so later, we found he was counting. He had done four sweats already and only needed nine hundred ninety-six more. He would learn later that the Spirits decide if one is to be a medicine man. As far as I know, he was never chosen.

It is important to know that traditional medicine people never charge for a ceremony. Tobacco is the only tool of commerce. A simple pouch of tobacco is all that is necessary. I spent seven intensive years with White Wolf and he never charged me a dime. I helped in many ways, but there was never a charge.

CHAPTER 19

MOON CUSTOMS

Moon customs can be an obstacle for many people, but is important to understand the power of the moon and the reason why moon customs are observed around all of the big three ceremonies.

A woman's menstrual period is what Natives call her moontime. When around an Indian camp, you will hear, regarding any approaching ceremony, that Moon customs will be observed. A woman in her period does not participate in these ceremonies.

Often modern, non-native women can get very angry about these restrictions. They think that this is just another example of men trying to control women. While that may be true in other situations, it has nothing to do with moon customs.

There are subtle changes happening in a woman's body and psyche during this time. We are so bombarded with energies and electromagnetic impulses twenty four hours a day, so overwhelmed with noise and static, that men and women are rarely aware of the subtle energies at work in their bodies. Women, because of their relationship with Grandmother Earth and Grandmother Moon, have more of these energetic influences. It is no accident that the moon cycle is twenty eight days.

Moontime has nothing to do with cleanliness or uncleanness. This is not a Judeo-Christian concept. Women in their moon are experiencing a reversal of their usual energies. The moon time energies are, of necessity, destructive energies, not in an evil sense, but in true physiological clearing away of uterine tissues. This is a normal and healthy process. The inipi and pipe ceremonies work with energies just the opposite of moontime energies. Both energies are important but should not be mixed in ceremony.

In Native communities, men aren't involved in moon custom practices. They are not even supposed to be aware of all this. It is a concept for and by women. A brilliant young man in Whitewolf's camp persisted in asking Whitewolf to explain why women couldn't be in the inipi ceremony if they were in their moontime.

Whitewolf kept telling him that he didn't know why, but that was the way it was. Finally, exasperated, Whitewolf said, "Don't bother me with this again. If you have to know, go ask some old Indian Grandma to tell you."

Later the young man married into a traditional, matriarchal tribe. During a visit to his wife's reservation a big healing ceremony was scheduled. The whole extended family including the tribal grandmother was there. He saw his chance. Approaching the old matriarch, he said, "Grandmother, can we talk?"

"Certainly," she said. Retiring to a private area, she asked, "What is it, grandson?"

He replied, "I have been well taught about the ceremonies and I know that women in their moontime cannot do the inipi, but my teacher couldn't tell me why. He said I should ask an elder Grandmother. So, I am asking you."

She looked him straight in the eye and said, "Grandson . . . that is none of your business!"

It is not men's place to understand this or teach it. Women, if they are sensitive enough, know the energetic changes that occur monthly. They are in sync with Grandmother Earth in a way that men could never understand. What I know of this has come from my wife, who was taught these things by the Spirits while on her three day/three night vision quest.

CHAPTER 20

SMUDGING

Red Path Zen ceremonies begin with smudging, bathing the body in the smoke of prairie sage. If the ceremony is to take place indoors, we often will do the smudging outside. Otherwise, we might set off fire alarms or cause allergic reactions among some participants. Usually the prairie sage is rolled into a ball, placed in a sea shell or small bowl, lit, and fanned over the participant. It can be bought in many New Age stores as a sage wand and waved around the person. Some of the wands also contain flat cedar and sweet grass. All these herbs are used ceremonially.

The smudge smoke smells suspiciously of marijuana. In 1978 I was hired as executive director of the Tri-County Youth Services Bureau in southern Maryland. I was excited by the new job. It offered a great place to work, the staff seemed quite competent, and the clinical director was fully occupied setting up an excellent training and accountability program.

After I was there about a week, the administrator came into my office. She said, "Dr. Duncan, the secretarial staff are concerned. They say you are smoking dope in your office every morning. You need to talk to them."

Laughing, I explained that they were smelling smudge smoke. According to native teachings, sage smoke drives away anything that is unclean. It purifies the air around us. In modern parlance, it settles the vibes. I cleaned my office and therapy rooms each morning with smudging.

In Michigan, our sangha meets in a location that offers Chinese healing modalities, Qi Gong, and martial arts training. We were preparing for our evening sangha. Priscilla was outside smudging everyone. A lady came down the sidewalk, and Priscilla, thinking she was a sangha member, immediately began to fan the smoke over her. She broke into a run, crying: "Stop that. Don't do that." She wasn't part of the group and Priscilla nearly scared her to death. She couldn't imagine what that strange woman was trying to do to her.

There are other kinds of sage that are available. There is white sage and culinary sage. The latter is never used in native ceremonies but occasionally found in some New Age ceremonies. Both have strong smells, but I personally don't like them for smudging. Some people do, and that is perfectly okay for them.

Once, when Priscilla and I were driving out west on the Apache Reservation, we came upon a patch of sage growing beside the road. It looked right. It had a kind of smell to it, so we picked a bunch and took it home to Whitewolf, thinking we were making a real contribution to the community. He laughed at us and told us it was Horse Sage and was really good for nothing. What a disappointment but a good learning for us.

Sacred sage can be ordered via the internet, bought in wand form, or grown in your own garden. It is not culinary or white sage. The closest thing you can grow is Artemisia Silver Queen (not Silver King). Grow it. Harvest it. Dry it. Use it.

CHAPTER **21**

TOBACCO CEREMONIES

Far, far back in the dim ages of human beings, people lived in a sacred way as best they understood. They sensed that there were practices that would enhance their ability to pray. Archeologists have found evidence of religious ceremony such as ritualized burials. We can imagine that they longed for a way to give back to the Creator, to express gratitude and wonder. But what did they have that the Creator needed? What could they give?

The Spirits had pity on them and gave them an herb that we know as tobacco, and said: "When you pray, use this." We think this was how tobacco became the sacred herb of the people. That early to-bacco had a real kick to it. The closest thing to the earliest form is Nicotina Rusticana.

When you want to give a gift of respect to a holy man, or you want to request a sacred ceremony, you give a pouch of tobacco. Since we don't usually have Nicotina Rusticana, give the purest form you can find. Avoid tobacco that is seasoned with alcohol. A tradi-tional Indian ceremonialist will not charge or take money for a sacred service. You cannot buy Native religion. You give tobacco.

My closet is full of tobacco. Periodically, I take all the tobacco, pour it into a large metal bowl, mix it with certain sacred herbs (no funny stuff), and prepare what we call sacred tobacco. This then is put in plastic bags and dispersed to other pipe carriers in the community.

There is a simple tobacco prayer ceremony. It is especially appropriate at sunrise but can be performed at any time of day. While not listed as among the major Lakota ceremonies, it is a lovely traditional ceremony that I first learned from Rolling Thunder, a Cherokee Shoshone medicine man.

Build a sacred fire. Start by asking the Spirits to help you and bless what you are doing. Collect some dry tinder or fat wood, but never use paper. Have some larger pieces of wood nearby. Put some tobacco on the wood and light the fire. Add other wood as necessary. You don't need a large fire, just enough to last until the ceremony is finished. Add another pinch of tobacco to honor the fire spirit.

If you are the only one, stand facing the sun across the fire, and if you know any sacred sunrise songs, sing them. If not, stand quietly and let yourself move into mindfulness. When you are ready, take a pinch of tobacco, hold it at eye level, and make your prayer. When you are finished, still holding the tobacco, trace a sun-wise circle with your hand, lifting it to the sky and lowering it toward the earth. Drop the tobacco into the fire. The old people say that the smoke carries your prayers to the Sacred Mystery. Offer thanks to the Spirits for hearing your prayer, and finish by saying, "Mitakuye Oyas'in" or (All My Relations.)

Let the fire burn itself out. Do not extinguish the fire with water unless it is necessary to prevent the fire from escaping. Some years ago a sweatlodge fire got away from the fire tender and burned about 30 acres on the reservation. Always be careful, but if possible, let the fire burn itself out.

CHAPTER **22**

THE CHANUPA WAKAN (SACRED PIPE)

The one ceremony that is becoming more accessible is the sacred pipe ceremony. It is at the heart of all our native ceremonies. Whatever sacred event a native spiritual community is observing, the chanupa wakan is most always involved.

Here is the story of how the chanupa wakan came to the Lakota people nineteen generations ago.

Indian people had a clear understanding of what it meant to be human beings. There was no value to rugged individualism, the "me first" attitudes so often shown by White folk. Indians were a communal people who took care of each other.

So it was that when hunters came home with a buffalo or antelope, the best cuts were given to the chiefs, medicine men, elders, widows, children, orphans, and others who could not hunt for themselves. You gave to others first, and then fed yourself. The Lakota had always followed the precept of generosity.

They had lived a difficult existence for centuries as they were pushed around by other tribes. Ultimately, they found themselves on the great plains, where they discovered the horse.

The horse made all the difference. With it they became great hunters and warriors. They were fierce. Other tribes called them "Sioux" which meant "cut throats." They became so successful that they forgot how to be human beings. The elders, widows, and orphan were neglected. Hunters would even kill game for target practice and leave the remains to rot on the prairie. The tribe fell out of balance.

During the fall of each year, the people would prepare food to last the winter. They knew that the game would disappear, but it always returned in the spring. Typically, the people would work hard making pemmican (a mix of dried buffalo, dried chokecherries, and such other berries as they could find). But also typically, they would not make quite enough so that by the time the game returned, the people would be hungry.

Imagine the despair of the Lakota when the arrival of Spring did not bring back the buffalo, the elk, the deer. . .not even a rabbit. Day after day, hunters returned empty handed, and the people began to starve. The very young and old were dying. It was Creations way of jerking awake the tribe that had lost its way.

One morning two brothers went hunting. All morning they searched for anything that could feed even one person. They did not see a rabbit or a bird, let alone an antelope or deer. The world was still.

The brothers approached the crest of a hill and knew that just beyond was a valley. Perhaps they would see something. As they inched forward on their bellies so that they would not frighten any game, they raked the valley with their eyes.

Then suddenly, they noticed movement on the hillside across from them. What was it? As their eyes adjusted, they saw that it was a woman making her way down to the valley floor.

One of the brother said, "That's a woman and she is alone. I am going to go take her."

His brother answered, "You better leave her alone. She may be Wakan (sacred)."

"Nonsense," the first brother replied, and he began to scramble down the hill thinking that if he couldn't find game to eat, he at least found another game for the taking.

As he approached the woman, she signaled him to come on. You can imagine how exciting this was for him. The woman was willing.

He ran up to her. The other brother was watching from his perch on the hilltop. Suddenly, the woman and the young hunter were enveloped in a fog. When the fog dissipated, the woman stood there. At her feet was a skeleton with all manner of unclean things crawling through it.

She looked up toward the other brother and signaled him to come down to her. He didn't know whether to run or obey. Obviously, she was sacred, so he decided to obey her. She told him to return to his village and tell Chief Standing Hollow Horn that in four days she would be there, that she had something for the people. She said to tell the Chief to bring all the people together.

The young man ran all the way to the village. Breathlessly he described all that he had seen and heard. Immediately the chief sent runners to the outlying villages. The next morning you could see the dust of hundreds of tipis being dragged to the Chief's Village.

A large, council tipi was constructed, and the people waited. On the fourth day, the woman arrived and went straight into the large tipi followed by the chiefs and head men. The sides were rolled up so that all the people outside would be able to watch what was about to happen.

The woman began to teach the people the seven sacred rites of the Lakota. When she had finished she said:

"One more thing before I leave. The Great Mystery is pleased with the way you have prayed with sacred tobacco. Now, He is giving you an altar upon which to burn that tobacco."

She unwrapped a bundle that she had brought with her. Inside was a Buffalo Pipe. She taught them how to use it, how to protect and honor it She told them that as long as they honored the Pipe and lived like human beings with each other, famine would never come to the people again.

Placing the Pipe Bundle in the chief's hands, she walked out of the council tipi and out onto the prairie. Suddenly she was hidden in a fog. When it dissipated, a white buffalo calf was rolling in the dust. It jumped up and gamboled over the horizon. The woman is known as the White Buffalo Calf Maiden.

Stone for making chanupas is found at Pipestone National Monument in Pipestone, Minnesota. Only Indians can mine that stone. All of our pipes have come from that mine, and all of our pipes are One with that original Buffalo Chanupa, which is still held by the Lakota People in a special place on the Cheyenne River Reservation in South Dakota. Orvol Looking Horse is the nineteenth generation Sacred Pipe Keeper meaning that the Buffalo Calf Woman brought the pipe to us nineteen generations ago. In each generation there has been a keeper of the Pipe. When Looking Horse dies, another will take his place.

To the best of our abilities, we use the chanupa wakan in the same way that the Buffalo Calf Woman taught. One doesn't just buy a pipe and become a pipe carrier. One must be part of a community where the pipe is held and used by an individual who was authentically trained. In Red Path Zen we carefully observe all the rules about its use and care.

The pipe ceremony is very powerful. It is a primary connection to the Sacred. It is key for healing, for teaching, visioning, for contacting the Spirits. In our Red Path Zen Sanghas, the pipe is taught in the right way and used only if there is an appropriately trained pipe carrier present, and moon customs are observed.

I will not describe the way the pipe ceremony is done lest someone decide to become a pipe practitioner based on these words. But, here is the meaning of the pipe:

The bowl is made of red pipestone from Pipe Stone National Monument in Pipestone, Minnesota. It comes out of the ground like soapstone, soft enough to be shaped and polished. There are many forms and decorations on the pipe bowl, but all can be used for sacred ceremonial purposes. The bowl is mineral. The pipe stem is made of wood, usually a soft wood like sumac that can be easily drilled and shaped. It is vegetable. On the stem you will most always find buckskin, and in the case of a ceremonial pipe, it may well have eagle feathers on it. Thus in the pipe, you have animal, vegetable, and mineral. Fitting the stem and bowl together you unite male and female. When you fill it with the sacred tobacco mix, you hold the whole world in your hand. The people refer to the filled pipe as a "loaded" pipe, because it carries the power of the universe.

If you have the opportunity to join a pipe ceremony, take off your shoes and the leader will direct you in how to participate.

CHAPTER **23**

THE INIPI (SWEATLODGE)

Lakota myth teaches that the White Buffalo Calf Woman gave the sweatlodge ceremony to the people. The particular form and meaning of the Lakota ritual may have come from Her, but the sweatlodge has been part of Native culture and religion as far back as archeology can take us. It is the oldest religious practice on this continent so far as we know. I have no doubt that some ceremonies may be older, but we have archeological proof of the inipi.

Not only is it part of indigenous religious practices, there were sweatlodges in Ireland (I have seen an ancient one). The Scandinavian Sauna was originally a purification sweat ceremony and in the Michigan Upper Peninsula, there is a Finish community that still has the ancient, sacred sauna songs.

So when we approach the inipi we are connecting to ancestors of all native people even as we are purified and connected to Mitakuye Oyas'in. . .the whole creation.

The inipi is approached with great respect and commitment. It is a work-intensive ceremony. A brief description of the lodge itself was given earlier in this book. The hard work of preparation is done with appreciation for the purification to be received.

On the day of the inipi, you must not partake of any alcohol or illicit drugs. You come dressed to work, for wood must be gathered, cut, and split. The lodge may need to be covered. There is much to do.

Next, the fire tender must select the number of stones to be used. That number will be dictated by the sweatlodge leader and will be based on outside temperature. More stones will be used in winter than in summer, for instance. You will be impressed by the prayerful way in which the stones are selected.

A wooden platform is built in the fire pit. The stones are prayerfully arranged on the platform. Four small poles representing the four Grandfathers (directions) will be leaned on the stones. Then, firewood will be placed around the stones in a sun- wise (clockwise) direction. When finished, you have a wooden tipi over the stones. Tobacco is offered and the fire prayerfully set.

As the fire burns, participants make tobacco ties. Each community has its own number to be made. In mine, we use sixteen ties that represent the sixteen faces of the Sacred. It is also the sacred number of four multiplied by four. The ties are very small pouches of tobacco tied onto crochet string. Into each tie, a prayer is made.

There is a lot of time for teaching, laughing, and enjoying ourselves while the stones heat. This process takes several hours. As the time to sweat draws closer, the pipe carriers fill their chanupas and lean them against the buffalo skull altar. When the stones begin to glow red, everyone dresses for the lodge.

Men wear beach towels while women wear a dress made of two towels sewn together. I have only been in one sweat ceremony where some of the participants were nude. Indians are very earthy and natural people, but also modest.

The inipi ceremony is divided into four rounds. In the first round, we call the Grandfather of all the directions to be with us and welcome all the Spirit teachers. The lodge becomes quite crowded. A lodge usually holds about ten to twelve people, while the Grandfathers require no physical space at all. Songs appropriate to each round are sung.

After the first round, the door flap opens and everyone takes a bit of water and cools down from the heat.

The second round offers everyone a chance to pray aloud. Over time a real sense of trust and community grows, so that the prayers become very strong and real. Once, there was a Jesuit Priest in Whitewolf's lodge. He was a fine young man. It was not unusual for a Priest to be in the lodge. There is nothing in our practices that would offend Christian sensibilities. When the second round came, the young priest prayed, "Hau, Grandfather. I ask you to help me with my temptations toward women."

The round continued. From the darkness at the back of the lodge we heard, "Grandfather, I ask that you take those temptations away from Father Bill." After which, the young priest quickly prayed, "Oh no, Grandfather. Don't take them away, just help me deal with them."

We always thought he was a very wise priest.

The third round is called the Pipe Round and this is the time for the medicine person, if one is present, to offer healing or to get the Spirits help in answering questions or meaning of dreams. If no medicine person is available, this is a time for general healing prayers. The lodge is by nature a healing ceremony.

The fourth round is reserved for the water pourer to make his/her own prayers. Others may also offer additional prayers.

At the end of the inipi, all the sacred pipes are smoked in the lodge, one at a time. Every one emerges from the lodge, ringing wet, dirty, but purified in body, mind and spirit.

At the time of this writing, there are only two sweatlodges open to Red Path Zen folk. They are traditional Lakota sweats. The time will come when there will be followers of Red Path Zen who will be authentically trained to offer the inipi.

CHAPTER **24**

HANBLECHEYA (VISION QUEST)

Hanblecheya means "crying for a vision," or vision quest. Crying is a common part of this event because it is physically hard and emotionally wearing. It is a scary time when you ascend the hill alone to face the Grandfathers. There are variations in the way it is done, but this is the way I learned from Whitewolf.

There are all kinds of vision quests performed by New Age groups. I believe that Outward Bound and similar groups also do them. No doubt all of these practices are useful. Any time western people walk away from their electronic connections and interact with the Creation face to face, I think it can only be good. The Native American vision quest is more difficult.

To go on the hill, our name for vision questing, one must first be a pipe carrier. That means he or she will have been part of a ceremonial community long enough to assume some responsibility and to be given a sacred pipe. You wouldn't want to go on the hill without your pipe to guide, encourage, and protect you.

You must ask the Spirits through your medicine person if it is time for you to go. If They say, "yes," then you set the date with the medicine person and give yourself at least six months to get ready.

With a date set, usually in the summer, your dread and excitement begins to build.

You greet the sun every morning with a pipe ceremony. During the last couple of months you fast food and water for periods of time to begin to toughen yourself for the coming ordeal.

In the final week, you string 100 tobacco ties of the color of each direction and wrap these around a piece of cardboard so they won't get tangled. By this time you have acknowledged that people sometimes do not come back from vision quest, so you make sure your will is up to date and that you have your life in order.

The first time you vision quest, it will usually be for one day and a night. You have no food or water and no human contact once left on the hill. You stand in a ten foot by ten foot area demarcated by the tobacco ties. You stay there for your time without leaving unless you need to answer nature's call to a pit nearby. You never want to leave the altar because inside it, you are safe. However, if you must leave, there is a way to do so without breaking the protection given by your altar and chanupa wakan.

There are evil Spirits in the universe. They will do you harm. Most of the time we do not have anything they would want, and so they are not attracted to us. However, when you are in a most holy and sacred space, like a vision quest altar, you are like a lightning rod attracting Them. So long as you remain in the altar, you are safe.

The second time you go up on the hill, you know what to expect. Because of that you are even more frightened than the first time. You are without food, water or shelter for two days and two nights. Most people will only do one vision quest; a few will do two. You often get your sacred name and medicine animals on your first vision quest. The second may add to that. A three day/three night vision quest is very hard and dangerous, and only someone called to the Medicine road will attempt a four day/four night vision quest.

There are certain ritual acts that you perform during the vision quest, but mainly you are to observe everything. Be aware. Pay attention. See and remember everything.

When I came down from my first vision quest, I told Whitewolf everything I could remember. He kept asking me, "Is that all? Are you sure?"

I told him that I couldn't remember anything else. He said that the Spirits told him there was something else very important. If I remembered it, I should mention it in the next sweat. As I talked with Whitewolf later, I said there just wasn't anything of importance, except one little black butterfly that hung out in the altar area with me. He laughed and said that was probably it.

During the next sweat, I mentioned the butterfly. The Spirits told me that after the sweatlodge, I was to take my pipe, go back up the hill to my spot. I was to sit down and hold my pipe. They said the butterfly would come to me. I was to take it and bring it to Whitewolf who would know what I should do

It happened exactly that way. I filled my pipe and ascended the holy hill. Once there, I sat down holding my chanupa wakan with the stem pointed to the west. Before long, the little butterfly came, circled my pipe stem a couple times, and landed on the pipe just below my hand. I thanked him, grasped him gently, and returned to Whitewolf.

Only people with a real question will go up for the third time, three days and nights with no food or water or shelter. You can imagine how hard this is. You stop being hungry, but your body cries for water.

On the last night of my three day/three night, a line of severe thunderstorms passed over me. With no moon or stars, the night was black as velvet. Then lightning flashes would blind me for a second or two. As the storm built, lightning burst all around me. I could smell the ozone. I stood on the top of the hill, sacred pipe in my hand, begging for mercy when it suddenly hit me that I was the tallest thing around. I dropped to the ground in a fetal position, hands clamped on my pipe . . . and then I was gone.

I didn't know what happened, but when I opened my eyes, the night was still. The storm had gone. I had survived. It was a year later during my four day/four night hanblecheya that I learned the lightning had knocked me out and the Spirits had chosen me to be a Heyoka (trickster) type spiritual person.

As soon as the time on the hill is finished, you go into the sweat immediately. During the ceremony you recount everything you have seen. The Medicine Man will take your report to the Spirit World and will find out what it all means.

To conduct someone on a vision quest, one must be able to pour water for the sweatlodge and also communicate with the Spirits at least at Level two. Since I am no longer allowed to pour water, I cannot conduct. I must trust that Spirit will someday bring us a Red Path Zen priest who is equipped to do this ceremony.

CHAPTER 25

THE URGENCY OF OUR TIMES

Change is in the air. Wherever you turn, you can feel it, the excitement, the apprehension. All the tribal prophesies of which I am aware, are foretelling the end of the age. The Hopis, respected keepers of prophecy among the Indian nations, are very clear that we are at the end of the Fourth Age and on the threshold of the new. Then, there is the Mayan calendar that has been so accurate for the last millennia. It ended December 21, 2012. The current age is merging into a new challenging period. What did 2012 portend? Where are we now?

Not only are Indians living in end-of-age anxiety. Scientists have joined the dismal chorus with their warnings about climate change and its disastrous effects for Grandmother Earth. The effects are evident all around us. We may have reached the tipping point beyond which restoration for Grandmother Earth is impossible. I believe that She will recover, but our species may not.

The Grandmother, and we, by extension, are facing a terrible crisis. It would seem that Her human children in their greed and excess have no concern for Her or any of their sibling nations: The trees, waters, plants, four leggeds, winged ones, fins, and all others too numerous to list. We continue to burn coal without scrubbing the smoke of contaminants. We wallow in fossil fuels with all the concomitant pollution. Many people still deny there is a relationship between fossil fuels and global warming, but 99.9 percent of world scientists and careful research studies clearly tell us that the world is warming and that humans are at least partially responsible. Already, we are experiencing extreme weather events that are related to climate change.

The traditional Hopi "elderly elders, men and women in their 90's and 100's," have opened their prophetic teachings to everyone. Several books are available, but I would recommend Thomas Mails' *The Hopi Survival Guide*, which was written with the help of one of the few surviving traditional elders, Dan Evehema, a 103 year old man (at the time when his book was begun). The Hopis teach that we are at the end of the Fourth Age or cycle of the earth and one small step into a new age of Hope and Oneness. This teaching is in accordance with prophecies of other tribes.

Some of the Hopi prophecies have already happened. The prophesies foretold that there would be roads in the sky; there would be moving Houses of iron; there will be Horseless carriages; that someday we would speak through "cob webs" in the sky; and that we would speak through space.

They predicted World Wars I and II and said that WWII would end with a gourd of ashes being poured on the earth (the atomic bomb). They warned that there would be a final world war. There would be another gourd of ashes that would burn brighter than the sun. The prophecies said that Hopi elders should go four times to the House of Mica (The UN) on the east coast to speak with the leaders of the nations. They have already done this but have never been received in a serious way by the UN. All the signs and prophecies tell us that the age has turned, and it is up to us to see that the promise of a new age of Oneness comes to pass.

According to the Hopi, we should look for the following signs: Changing seasons and weather patterns; geological unrest; unusual volcanic activity; strange animal behavior. Do you recognize any of this?

The polar ice caps are melting at an alarming rate. The North Pole now reveals open water during the summer. Polar bears are dying because they can't reach the prey necessary for their lives. Animals are leaving Yellowstone. The natural world is in upheaval and change because of global warming. Just today (January 2013) I tried to buy artichokes at the supermarket and was told that they aren't being harvested because of the unusually cold weather in California and the southwest. Other vegetables are also in short supply already because of climate change.

These are not isolated situations. Every facet of our ecosystem is under stress from the forests of Brazil, where hundreds of thousands of acres of forests are being clear cut, to the tundra of Alaska where the oil barons are determined to drill and destroy.

Ten summers ago, my daughter, Laura Smokes, was on a vision quest. She was shown a huge turtle with a crack running from the top to the bottom of the shell. On either side of the turtle were two people, one wearing a bear headdress, the other a buffalo headdress, and they were fighting over the turtle. Following behind was a person with his arms stretched out toward the turtle. The Spirits told her that the crack in the shell means that the turtle continent/earth is broken. The people fighting over the pieces didn't necessarily represent Whites and Indians; they represented people with conflicting agendas for the land. The person following behind stood for all of us who are trying to prevent the crack from becoming permanent. Smokes was told that it was not known if we can heal the crack, but that we must keep trying.

I took my sacred pipe and asked the Grandfathers what to expect as we transition into the coming age. The response was so vivid. It was like watching a movie. I saw war scenes of great magnitude. I was told that the whole Middle East would go up in flames. The USA would be drawn into the conflict. Our leadership would deny the use of nuclear bombs but would admit to tactical nuclear weapons. Such weapons would be used on all sides. In the meantime, there would be two dirty bombs exploded in the US and more in Europe.

With all the expense of the wars, and the chaos wrought here, Europe, and the rest of the world, the international economy will collapse. As I write this, both the American and European economies are teetering. There will be many lives lost from war, hunger, and illnesses of various kinds. The positive side of this horror is that the world population of human beings will be seriously lowered allowing Grandmother to survive as a home for All Our Relations.

It is a hard vision, but we know that the death of the old age must come if there is to be the birth of the new. Death precedes birth. For the past three or four years there has been a growth of consciousness among human beings. More and more of us are beginning to see how we are inter-related and how we must become "family" to survive. Out of the chaos this consciousness will move to fruition. The new age will see real changes in human attitudes and awareness. Right now it looks very grim. The old consciousness of greed and aggression still holds sway.

This is not a time for panic. A little dread is appropriate because survival will be difficult. Many among us may die, crossing over to life in another dimension. But these are exciting times as well. We are participating in an incredible movement from one world cycle to another. Those of you who are young enough to live the next twenty-five years, are going to see positive changes beyond your wildest dreams. 2012 and the years following will see an accelerated growth in our consciousness. Unfortunately, people caught in the old, destructive ways of thinking will continue to exert power, but their years are numbered. The time is coming when war will no longer be the status quo. There will be a slow but continuous growth in higher, spiritual consciousness among all people. Listening to the voices of our ancestors will no longer be a gift of the few.

We will eventually realize the dream of the world becoming a single tribe in which human beings will be actively concerned for each other and actively caring for each other. We will protect the Grandmother and all Her children from ravishment for dollars. Multinationals will not be allowed to steal the natural resources of the nations. Human beings will not be treated as slaves to make cheap goods. Corporations will be controlled in such a way that capital is used for the good of all people. The old, organized religious systems with their penchant for war and xenophobia will be replaced by true spirituality.

Sounds like utopia? Maybe. At least we can hope that in the coming age after all the conflict and chaos, human beings will move toward spiritual maturity. That is the promise. Together, we will face whatever comes. I hope that my vision of destruction never comes true but that the dream of a new, higher level of consciousness will be realized. Prepare yourself by deepening your own spirituality and understanding, and you will see the importance, the necessity of developing community among all our relations.

I offer these stories and teachings in the name of All My Relations, my Spirit Teachers, and my Zen Ancestors. May they be a blessing to all Creation.

Mitakuye Oyas'in,
Rev. Grandfather Duncan Sings-Alone, Sensei

CHAPTER 26

POSTSCRIPT

Never anticipate the Spirits. They operate with Their own time tables and agenda. Four years ago they dragged my reluctant body from the inipi to make sure that I put my energy into teaching Non-Indians. I was led to Zen Buddhism where I established Red Path Zen within the Zen Garland Order. Significant energy and plenty of ink has been spilt over my angst at not being able to sweat. But, I did as I was asked.

Shortly after this book was completed, it occurred to me that I now had three Red Path Zen Sanghas. I was doing everything asked of me. Maybe now I could go back to the sweatlodge. Taking my chanupa wakan to vision quest hill, I pleaded my case.

To my surprise They said, "Yes. You are doing the work. You are training pipe carriers within Red Path Zen. Now you may start teaching your pipe people to pour water (lead inipi). You should not build a sweatlodge community in the traditional sense. Keep your teaching within Red Path Zen. The sweatlodge at your house remains with your daughter, Atsila Gaia. If you want to use it, ask first. You may also lead sweats for her at her discretion."

I was both excited and puzzled. They had agreed for me to pour water again, but sent me off in a new direction. I could run sweats, but it had to be within the Red Path Zen context unless I was asked by Atsila Gaia to pour water for her.

Coyote stepped carefully onto my zabuton (meditation mat). He stretched, front and back, canine fashion, yawned, circled twice and settled down for a nap. Raising an eyelid, he gave me a sly wink. I didn't know whether to laugh or fret. But, for now, I have my marching orders.

Aho! Mitakuye Oyas'in
Rev. Grandfather Duncan Sings-Alone, Sensei

CPSIA information can be obtained at www.ICGtesting.com
Printed in the USA
BVOW08s1753271013

334744BV00001B/1/P